Preface.

HIS volume has no claim to be considered, nor does it profess to be, one of learning or of research. It is but a simple record of my first impressions among strange habits and places, in a part of the kingdom which is seldom visited by tourists. After a somewhat lengthened residence on the Continent, it was by mere chance that, in search of health, I wandered hither. My stay was like that of the well known traveller in the East, who accompanied a friend to Calais, and remained abroad eighteen years. I came for two or three weeks, and stayed three months. The beauty of the Islands, and the kindness I received at all hands, made those three months the happiest I ever spent in my life. I have, in this work, attempted some return—though a poor one—for the pleasure I enjoyed; relating only what came under my own observation; and wishing the good Scillonians no happier lot than a continuance of their present blessings, under the same wise and paternal rule.

CONTENTS.

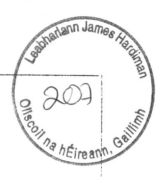

Scilly and its Legends.

BY

THE REV. H. J. WHITFELD, M.A.,

LATE OF DOWNING COLLEGE, CAMBRIDGE:
VICAR OF GRANBOROUGH, BUCKS;
AND DOMESTIC CHAPLAIN TO THE EARL OF MORNINGTON.

Æstuat, infelix, angusto in limite regni.
Ut Siluræ clausus scopulis, parvaque Minalto.

Facsimile reprint 1992
by Llanerch Publishers,
Felinfach.
ISBN 0947992847

Penzance:
PRINTED AND PUBLISHED BY F. T. VIBERT, MARKET-PLACE.

London:
SIMPKIN, MARSHALL, AND CO.

—

1852.

To Augustus Smith, Esq.,

TRESCO ABBEY,

LORD PROPRIETOR OF THE ISLANDS OF SCILLY.

My dear Sir,

I dedicate to you this little Book, not only in gratitude for your kindness, but from admiration of the manner in which you have raised these beautiful Islands from a state of misery into one of prosperity and comfort; reforming wisely, but cautiously; developing their resources with a firm and practical hand; and acting in the true spirit of your motto,—

" Preignes haleine. tire fort."

Believe me,

Your's obliged, and very truly,

H. J. WHITFELD.

Tresco,
June 16, 1852.

Scilly and its Legends.

CHAPTER I.

A FEW months since, when on my way hither, I read a very clever little work entitled " Rambles beyond Railways." Its author, Mr. Wilkie Collins, described with much spirit, before the feeling of novelty had worn off, his early impressions of the far West, and his extreme surprise and amusement at many things which he saw and heard. Indeed, as soon as he was well in this old realm of Cornwall, he found himself in a marvellous strange land. Every thing was new and striking. He was no longer in the England of yesterday. There, a pedestrian who paid his way handsomely was treated accordingly. Here, boys gaped after him, and their parents called him a " trodger;" landlords regarded him with a suspicious air, holding him to be a low sort of road surveyor; chambermaids asked him whether he was too good to sleep with a sheet above, and a blanket below, like other folks.* He inquired his way, and was directed to a road that led along

* The same question was put to me.

the top of a hedge. In one place, he saw a mystery of the
dark ages, performed in a ruined Roman amphitheatre. In
another (Helston) he encountered the antique Pagan Floralia,
under the corrupted name of *"furry dance."** At a mine,
he was treated as a mere Saxon younker, tucked under the
arm of a huge miner, and called " my son." In short, after a
long and charming excursion, he recorded its occurrences
for the delight of his readers, and left Cornwall fully per-
suaded that it was at least a century behind the rest of the
world; that stokers, and engineers, and buffers, were, and
would long be, as much matter of faith, as much a myth, as
piskies† are now to its peasantry; and that, for many a year,
its pleasant vales were to be spared the desecration of the
signal whistle. " Surely," he thought, " rambles beyond
railways shall still be a great fact! May distant Cornwall
preserve inviolate her clotted cream, her junket, her heavy
cake, her figgy pudding, and her savoury fish pie!"

Alas, for the vanity of human wishes! Six months afterwards I too wandered in the track of Mr. Wilkie Collins,
as did poor Inglis in the footsteps of Don Quixote; but false
were all his fair prophecies! The hoarse roar of an engine
was before me, and I was seated comfortably in a first class
carriage of the railroad from Redruth, with a return ticket
in my pocket. I timed the distance from Marazion-road to
Penzance, as we flew by the shore of Mount's-bay. We did
it in four minutes. St. Michael's Mount looked grandly upon
us as we passed. Robert the Norman, son of the Conqueror,
once rode along those sands, and his beleagured brother

---

* Flora-day, or, Flurry-day.

† Piskies, Pixies, Devon, i. e. fairies. A man who loses his way at
night is said to be " piskie-led."

peered down upon him from the battlements above. There is a memory of the Druids about that " hore rock in the wood," as they then called it, before the sea had submerged the great plain that girded it in. King Charles the Martyr there held his latest court, amid the expiring pomp of royalty. Phœnicians, and Carthaginians, and Romans had, by turns, robbed and ruled around that stern old " Ictis: " and now we rushed past it with a careless glance, going thirty miles an hour, at the will and bidding of a grimy stoker, who was looking forward to an evening with his wife and six future stokers and stokeresses, and who did not care a groat for the associations and the beauties keeping their watch around. So far, therefore, there was an end of " rambles beyond railways." The steam giant had won the race. The romance of travel had retired farther westward. On the platform venerable gentlemen, unmistakeably of the Hebrew persuasion, were discussing the price of shares; polite officials, marked W.C.* on their collars, received and escorted you to the door; a railway omnibus bore you to a railway hotel; and when, on arriving, you took up the " Times," you found Cornwall no longer an unknown country, for you had its scrip quoted there.

There is something very disenchanting in this rude revulsion of place and scene. There is, as Lord Stowell called it, " a laceration of feeling " that is hard to bear. The beautiful and the rare are not of such frequent occurrence that we can afford to lose them thus easily, or to part from them without a pang. Our fancy may linger around a dream, in which it revels and believes, even while our reason fails to be con-

---

* West Cornwall.

vinced. So it was with the charm lent by distance to these far spots of earth, the old realms of Tristram and of King Mark. My imagination at least was no infidel; I trusted with a pious fondness in the accounts which I had heard and read, and which I had shadowed forth in my mind's eye, of these simple regions. It was very hard to find so many happy anticipations frustrated, to behold such an airy fabric of hope thus abruptly overthrown. The Atlantis I had come so far to see had sunk beneath the waves, and the common things of life took its place and rolled over its vanished beauties, as though it had never been.

While I was musing thus, a person by my side inquired from the waiter when the packet would sail for Scilly? The reply was " to-morrow morning, should wind and weather permit." " Is it not then," said I, " a steamer?" " No," answered the waiter, " no, sir, it is a sailing boat, that goes with the mails, twice a week, from Penzance." So there was actually, within the British dominions, a place, not only without a railway, but even without a steam packet. " Now," thought I, " I can have a ramble beyond railways; I will go over to Scilly to-morrow morning."

A friend of mine, during his residence in France, once fell in with an Abbé who had never left his native district, surviving there, in his inoffensive obscurity, the Revolution, the Empire, and several phases of Monarchy, for so great and so wise a people as the French cannot be expected to remain content with one kind, preferring a government, like a theatre, des varietés. My friend rallied the old man on his want of curiosity, that had kept him at home, but the worthy priest had a reply to his hand. " Ah!" he said, " vous voyagez beaucoup, vous autres Anglais, et pourquoi?

Moi aussi, par exemple, je voyage, mais c'est dans ma bibliotheque. Je veux savoir quelque chose à cause de l'Angleterre, je prends Cæsar, et qu'-y vois je? ' Londres—pas London, c'est un vilain mot, mais—Londres, grande ville, située sur la Tamise, pays barbare, gens cannibales.' Et voilá tout, et c'est assez pour moi."

I am already, thought I, in a land where a man who builds a wall is called " a hedger," and into which " Punch " never penetrates; but I am now about to venture into a pays barbare, a still wilder spot, into a spot fabulous and unexplored, the dwellers in which lately petitioned for a communication with England once in six weeks, and to which the lady of the chaplain went in the full persuasion that she would have to milk her own cow, and to perform all the usual little domestic offices entailed upon emigrants in the Australian bush, or amid the backwoods of Canada. There was a delightful vagueness and uncertainty in the future. A gentleman to whom I mentioned my intention advised me to take the coroner with me. I did not know but that a Phœnician bark might be moored to the pier, bearing " its dyed garments from Bozrah," and ready to take us venturers on the deep to those tin islands, with which they still carried on a ghostly traffic. I went at last to sleep, dreaming that I was on the deck of a stately galley, before a fair carved altar of bronze, upon which I offered a sacrifice of frankincense to Astarte, and to the Tyrian Hercules, for a prosperous voyage.

CHAPTER II.

O N the morning of Saturday, the twenty-seventh of March, 1852, I stood upon the old Quay, Penzance.

In my place, a Roman would have abandoned the enterprise. The Iron Duke would have grumbled and gone on. An ill omen had decidedly encountered us at the outset.

The good yacht Ariadne was lying at her moorings outside the basin for want of water to enter; her boat was waiting for the appearance of Capt. Tregarthen, with Her Majesty's mails. And in that boat was the presage of evil, which an ancient traveller would have turned aside to avoid.

A young woman of respectable appearance was sitting on one of the benches, and sobbing convulsively. Poor thing! she had good reason for her sorrow. She had been sent for to Scilly to meet her husband, the mate of a merchant vessel, who had arrived from abroad in bad health. She had believed him to be still alive, but one of the crew had incautiously told her that he was dead. It was a pitiful sight to see her in her first agony of grief. That long and tedious day passed away with a foot of lead for us, but what must it have been to her?

Nevertheless we were soon on board. After the first bustle and confusion we settled down into our places, the anchor was weighed, and the Ariadne, spreading out her wings to the light and fitful breeze, crept lazily along.

If there be in the British dominions a scene, the beauties of which would make a calm endurable, surely it would be here. I have travelled in many far lands beyond the sea, but I never saw a view more exquisite, nor one that gains on you more than this. The Cornish are justly proud of it. Catch a native, and the chances are that his first words, as you hold him between your finger and thumb, will be " Have you seen the Mount?" It is an object of universal worship, and woe betide the unlucky wight who renders not due homage to its claims. There it lay, proud and still, as of yore. Centuries have passed over it since the galleys of Richard of the Lion's heart lay on the very spot now occupied by us, and prepared to wrest it from the Earl of Mortaigne, his false brother, afterwards King John. And there it lay, solemn in its consecration of ages, the object of veneration scarcely less religious than was offered upon its altars, when the mystic cross,* upon which weeds and lichens never grew, was then worshipped, as it is still seen, upon its western slope; and when the blessing of St. Michael was supposed to come down upon those who journeyed hither to kneel and pray.

As we crept slowly on, we had before us as grand a panorama as fancy ever drew. On our left was Marazion,† where are the beautiful and admirably conducted schools,

---

* Probably produced by some acid, or other chemical appliance.

† The Mayor of Marazion is said to " sit always in his own light," from the peculiar position of his pew at Church.

built by Lady Mary Cole, as a memorial of her late husband,
Sir Christopher. Beyond, on the hill, rose the graceful spire
of St. Hilary; and Cudden point; and Prussia Cove, so
called from a smuggler nicknamed the King of Prussia;
and far away, in the dim distance, " the Lizard," the " Cabo
tormentoso " of the West.*

And so on we went, the sea around us crisped by the
breeze, and a fleet of mackerel boats adding life and interest
to the scene. Our skipper hailed one of them, and asked
what news? " A French boat took 70,000 mackerel into
St. Mary's " was the reply. A mail bag belonging to the
hapless Amazon was washed up yesterday at Newlyn, now
close by us; but it was a matter of no interest to the trawlers,
in comparison with a successful sweep of fish.

We passed in turns Mousehole, famous for the Spanish
blood, and for the beauty, of its women; and Lamorna Cove;
and Boscawen Carn, giving a name and title to the house of
Falmouth; and Boskenna, the ancestral seat of my excellent
and accomplished friend Mr. Paynter; and the famous
Logan Rock; and then came the Land's-end; and then the
everlasting deep, with its broad unwrinkled brow. The
tremendous power of ocean slumbered like a child. One
living thing only was in sight. It was the back fin of a
shark, that played around our bows. At last it dashed away
towards Penberth Cove, and we were alone upon the waves.

What a weary thing is a calm at sea! There, on our left

---

* " Cape of storms." When the news that Vasco de Gama had
doubled the Cape was brought to Alphonso of Portugal, according to
Camoens in the Lusiad,—

    " ' No Cape of storms ' the joyful king exclaimed,
    " ' Cape of Good Hope ' be thou for ever named."

hand, is the half-way mark between Penzance and Scilly, the Wolf—that is, the Gulf—rock, and we thought it never would come in sight, and then never would go out of it. We ought now to be at St. Mary's, and St. Mary's is a low dark speck upon our larboard bow, scarcely visible to the naked eye. The poor young widow had gone below, and cried herself, from sheer exhaustion, to sleep, while the rest of the passengers gathered together, and told dismal tales of passages extending over many days, and of the hardships thereby entailed upon unwary travellers, as the vessel carries no provisions.

At this moment we were joined by the Captain, a fine specimen of the English sailor. I asked him, in the course of conversation, if Hugh Town, the capital of the Islands, were considered a healthy place. "Healthy, Sir," replied he, "healthy, why of course it is, it must be healthy, it can't help it, for *there is so much water*." He told me, however, that the cholera never came there, and that though two persons with virulent small-pox once landed, the disease was confined to them, and spread no farther.

People certainly, as I hear, live to a great age at Scilly. The following extract is from the records of the Christian Knowledge Society.—

"Augustus Smith, Esq., Lord Proprietor* of the Scilly Islands, in a letter dated Penzance, April 13, 1852, informed the board of the death of Jacob Hicks, formerly a school-

---

* Mr. Smith is rightly named *Lord* Proprietor. In old Grants the Proprietors were called Lords Farmers, or Governors. He holds of the Crown, in fee, as a great vassal, and is, as it were, "per legem terræ," a Baron of England. So a Commoner is properly termed Lord Lieutenant, and we speak of a "Lord of the Manor."

master, and subsequently a pensioner of the Society. Mr.
Smith said that he died about a fortnight since, at the
venerable age of ninety-six, leaving, among other posterity,
a grandson, who had for some years been himself a grandfather."

It was dusk as we entered Crow sound, which is the
channel between the islands of St. Martin and St. Mary.
We were, even then, hardly certain of getting to our port
by night. I heard one of the passengers ask a sailor, very
querulously, if we were likely to reach Hugh Town before
Sunday morning. It was evidently not a matter of course
that we should sleep on shore. I don't know how the other
strangers were provisioned, but my sea stock was composed
of three captain's biscuits, and a paper of gingerbread nuts,
the kind parting gift of Mrs. Hampton, the confectioner, at
Penzance, to my children. Well, it could not be helped!
We bargained for novelty and romance, and, to a certain
extent, we had them. It was a trip beyond steamers, with a
vengeance!

Suddenly, at dusk, the sails began to fill, the Ariadne
drew more cheerily through the water, a few scattered lights
twinkled and danced upon a low line of coast before us, and
we found ourselves—literally at the eleventh hour—in port.

We were not, however, fated to leave our ship without one
other incident, to show that we were in a strange land. When
I went to pay my passage money, Captain Tregarthen would
not take it, and said he should see me somewhere again. He
was off with his mails before I could reply. With this
parting trait of primitive confidence, I went ashore, took
up my quarters at some very comfortable lodgings, in a
house where my attendant was a young lady who spoke

French, and meditated till bed-time on the subject of the following tale.*

---

* To those who are unacquainted with Cornwall, it may be necessary to say that the Islands of Scilly were supposed to have been formerly connected with the main land by a broad tract of country, called in Cornish "Lethowsow," or the "Lionesse" on which there were no fewer than 140 Churches. Tradition says that this wide and wealthy district was rent from the Land's-end, and submerged, by some violent convulsion. There is a curious confirmation of this legend, in the fact that flints and chalk formations, exactly similar, are found on the Castle downs at Tresco, and at the Land's-end, and are discovered there only, at the precise points where the islands and the continent face each other, and where the disruption—granting it to have occurred,—must have commenced.

CHAPTER III.

LETHOWSOW, OR THE LIONESSE.

NCE upon a time, long centuries ago, not only

> " Ere William led his Norman horde
> To plunder o'er the main,
> And the brave Saxon's patient sword
> Had yet expelled the Dane,"

but far back in those shadowy annals, which are at once so perplexing and so fascinating; through which we love

> " that glance to cast
> That lifts the veil and lives amid the past.
> To read high tales of virtue and of crime
> Robed in the dread magnificence of time,
> When error's beauteous mist forbids to scan
> The stern sad outlines of primeval man."

Long, long centuries ago, ere the Raven standard flew over our Isle; ere Hengist and Horsa came in as allies, and remained as masters; ere Britain ceased to belong to the British, the events occurred, which I have embodied in the following legend.

Those who have pored over the old romances of chivalry, and especially the goodly tomes of Syr Thomas Maleor, know well the state of things that existed during the reign of King Arthur. There is a charm in those rude days, an inexpressible charm, against which we struggle in vain. We see Arthur of Britain, drawing his good sword Excalibur from the enchanted stone, and Merlin, the Great Wizard, and the Round Table of Camelot, with its unrivalled knights. As they feast in hall, their forms rise up before us. We see Sir Kaye, the seneschal, whose high qualities were tarnished by his love for scornful jests; and Sir Bors de Ganis; and the noble Sir Ector de Maris; and Sir Caradoc, the husband of the fairest and most virtuous dame; and Sir Tristram, who loved too well the lady of his uncle, the false King Mark; and Lancelot of the Lake, the peerless warrior, over whose dead body it was said so beautifully,—" He was the kindest man that ever struck with sword; and he was the goodliest person that ever rode among the throng of knights; and he was the meekest man, and the gentlest, that did ever eat in hall among ladies; and he was the sternest knight to his mortal foe, that ever laid lance in rest." At the head of the board is Arthur, every inch a king, with his majestic presence, and his kindly smile. Nor was there wanting beauty at that royal banquet. Queen Guenever was there, regal in all respects save one, with her bright train. Alas! that those so lovely should shrink before the ordeal of virtue, and that one only of their number should dare to pledge the enchanted cup of gold, and to wear the embroidered robe.*

. In the days of my tale, the " terrors of Tintagel's spear"

---

* One day during a feast, a dwarf brought in a robe and a golden cup, and proclaimed that none but a virtuous dame could quaff from the one, or wear the other. The only lady of the Court who succeeded in doing so was the wife of Sir Caradoc. As Scott says—

> " And still those warriors fame survives
>   For faith so constant shown.
> There were two who loved their neighbours' wives,
>   And one who loved his own."

were yet existing, though the sway of the great monarch approached its close. Arthur was holding high court in his Castle of Tintagel, and around him were gathered his paladins, diminished indeed in numbers by long and bloody war, but still presenting an array that had never yet known reverse or defeat. The king was there, as usual, and at his right hand sate the queen, but the brow of Arthur was sad, and grew dark, when he marked the glances that passed between Guenever and Sir Lancelot. The spirit of the assembled knights was not what it was. There were among them empty seats; and they could not but remember that those places were not always void by death, but that even in that gallant company, treason had stolen in, and seduced some of those deemed the bravest and the best. High among the gathered nobles was an ominous gap, caused by the absence of Prince Mordred, and rumour spoke of evil designs, entertained by him against his kinsman and benefactor, even to the levying of open war. However, though changed from the frank courtesy and merriment of other days, the scene was, to the careless eye, splendid, and even gay. There was no lack of mirth, and song. Brave men whispered their homage to no unwilling ears; and soft cheeks waxed rosy, and wore a brighter charm, as the feast went on; and the royal brow of Arthur grew relaxed and lost its wrinkles, as he jested with the maidens of the queen; and though all was not as once it was, there was over all a semblance of enjoyment, and a careless bravery, that deceived the eye. If it were a counterfeit, it was a successful one. To those who did not look below the surface, the glory of the Round Table was untarnished, and the gaiety of its knights unimpaired.

When the feast was over, Arthur arose from his throne, and, taking in his hand a golden cup, pledged his guests as of yore. But when he lifted the chalice to his lips, a shudder passed over him, and he cast it from him with an action of horror and disgust. " It is not wine," he exclaimed, " it is blood. My father Merlin is among us, and there is evil in the coming days. Break we up our Court, my peers! It is no time for feasting, but rather for fasting and for prayer."

As he spoke he glanced anxiously and bitterly at the vacant stall of his cousin Mordred. It was no longer un-filled. A shadowy form seemed darkly to rest upon it. There was no distinct figure, no bodied phantom, but a vast dim likeness of something terrible, and strange. A cloudy spirit brooded over the traitor's seat. The assembly broke up in ghastly silence. They departed speechless and awe-struck. They went to pray against the ills to come.

These came, alas, too soon! Next morning arrived a weary post, with tidings of the revolt of Mordred. Then followed, day after day, fresh disasters. Foes banded together, and friends fell off. All whom the high handed king had put down and repressed, all from whom he had wrung ill gotten spoils, all with whom in fair fight he had contended for mastery, all false friends whom he had thought to buy with benefits, now leagued together against him. Single malcontents formed a band, and bands united swelled into an army. It advanced, with Mordred at its head, to strike a blow for the throne of Britain. All the while, Arthur lay still at Tintagel, and gave no sign of life. Perhaps he had lost somewhat of his early vigour. Perhaps he wished to give time to his enemies to declare themselves, that he might know on whom at last to rely. Perhaps he lingered in an agony of proud doubt, and indecision. But perhaps also, and it was most like the stout warrior, he disdained to show any apprehensions of a foe that he despised. Taking counsel only of his own kingly heart, he remained tranquil and undisturbed in his hold, looking down from thence upon the storm, as it came to a head in the plain below, and waiting for the proper hour to sally forth and scatter it.

It was still no child's play. The game was for an empire, and battles were to decide the cast. Nor were the players ill-matched; nor was it an " impar congressus Achilli." Those whom he was to meet in the coming war, were no longer rude Pagans or Soldans, clad in barbaric arms. They were the flower of his own chivalry, headed by a prince of his own blood. Together had they ridden through many a bloody field, and not a few of the champions opposed to him had slept under the same cloak, after a day of common danger. They had been trained beneath his experienced eye, and had learned the art of war under the guiding of his leading-staff. Many a one of them could say, in the expressive language of Scripture. " Remember how thou and I rode together after Ahab," and old times must surely have touched their hearts, when they saw in their front that banner, under which they had been so long victorious, and that well known leader, with his sad yet imperial glance, and his hair of silver sable, and his look, telling rather of sorrow than of years.

But rebellion has no shame. It grows more bitter for its very baseness, and fiercer for the badness of its cause. The array of Mordred pressed onwards in still increasing numbers. The land of Cornwall, never too friendly to Arthur, was alive with foes. They marched upon Tintagel, sternly, but slowly, for they had an instinctive dread of the old chief, as he lay grimly in his fastness, his renowned knights within its halls, his veteran levies around them, and in the centre of the whole, himself, a host, calm, unshaken, and resolute. They prepared to beard the lion in his den, but it was with secret misgivings that they did so, and many a heart that knew no other fear, faltered on its approach. And still Arthur never moved. It seemed as if he did not deign to parley with his revolted subjects. Their advanced guards and scouts might be descried from the donjon tower of the castle, but no movement followed the discovery. The main body was even seen, but the King lay stern and still.

Suddenly, at day-break one morning, the great bell of the fortress rang out a stirring peal, and before the barbican the trumpets sounded to horse, and all was bustle, and waving of pennons, and marshalling to arms. And in a short time Arthur rode out from the gate, followed by the mighty, who still adhered to him. There filed onwards the most renowned of his followers, Sir Lancelot, and Sir Tristram, Sir Banyan, and Sir Bor, Sir Ector, and Sir Cote mal taillé, Sir Caradoc, and Sir Percival, without a stain. They were the Fathers of the war, the chosen of Britain. They were men who

> " Would scorn, amid the reel of strife,
> " To yield one step for death or life."

And now, unconquerable, in proud defiance, they went forth to do battle for God and their king. Alone at their head was Arthur, with a brow of marble, collected and self-possessed. As he passed on, he issued his commands from

time to time, but his words were brief and stern, and he
never looked back. Men thought that the shade of Merlin
held communion with him. And so went forth Arthur to
his last of fields.

The next evening, a band of warriors was seen urging
their weary steeds across the wild heaths that were common
in Cornwall. Their course was in the direction of Cassiteris,
and of that fair wide tract of country called, in the Cornish
tongue, " Lethowsow." Their numbers were formidable,
amounting to several hundreds, but they were in no mood
nor condition for resistance, as was shown by their hacked
armour, and torn surcoats, and, in many instances, by the
blood that welled from their unstaunched wounds. They
hurried, for life and death, over the wastes before them. Not
a word was spoken. Now and then a straggler fell to the
rear from sheer exhaustion, but his absence in the disordered
ranks was unmarked. Sometimes they paused for a few
minutes at a brook or spring, suffered their horses to take a
hasty drink, tightened the saddle-girths, and were gone.
Their pace, as may be supposed, was not too quick, but they
made some progress, and when, as darkness fell, they drew
their reins, and prepared to encamp for the night, it was
after thirty miles sped over rough and broken roads. Glory
had apparently little to do with that tumultuous disarray.
Yet these jaded riders, flying before the face of their pursuer,
were all that remained of the chivalry of Britain. Arthur
lay dead upon the plain; the banner that had covered his
breast, until all was lost, was now borne, torn and bloody,
in the van. The survivors of that dreadful day were fleeing
for their lives, and Mordred thundered upon their rear.

They arose in the morning, and bouned them again for flight. Veterans as they were, the mere hardship of a rough ride and an unbroken fast was a trifle: they recked little of either. But disgrace and defeat were new and strange evils. These were the true bitterness of death. Nor could they altogether comprehend them, nor believe them as yet to be a sad and stern reality. They could attribute the dishonour that had tarnished their arms to no particular cause: there was no apparent reason for their fall. The stars in their courses had fought against them, and palsied their stout arms, and made their skill and valour vain. They brooded over these things as they rode on. They did not ponder deeply, for the recent shock had confused and rendered dull their ideas, but thoughts like these floated unconsciously through their brain. Arthur of Britain had gone down, and the best lances in the world were flying for their lives, with a conquering foe in hot chase after them.

The course of these waking visions was interrupted by the notes of a trumpet, which followed them with a prolonged wail through the air. Then it came louder, and yet more loud. They halted for a moment, and looked back. The veteran warriors could not brook to fly. They had submitted to misfortune: they could no longer bear disgrace. As they gazed, the air became radiant with the reflected light of steel, as shields, and morions, and lances, gleamed fitfully from the brow of a distant hill. It was the glimmering of the pursuer's arms. Should they make a stand and die? Should they condescend to purchase life by a farther retreat? There was the traitor, the murderer of his kinsman and sovereign. Should they not breathe their chargers, and await his coming, and strike one stroke for revenge?

While they paused, gloomy and irresolute, and gazed steadily at the advancing forces, there seemed to come between them a shadowy dimness, that assumed gradually the form of a gigantic figure. It was like a mountain mist, but yet it wore the shape and aspect of humanity. There was a likeness in its awful lineaments, a resemblance to one honoured and long departed, which the aged knights recognised at once. It was the awful ghost of Merlin! Like a sullen cloud, but yet instinct with the principle of life, it upreared its huge outlines between the spoilers and their prey, terrible in its indistinctness and with a supernatural and spiritual grandeur, rather felt than seen. It was a gulf between the two parties, impassable as that between the Egyptians and the flying Hebrews, and it troubled the following host, and checked them in their headlong speed. And so the chase continued. Sullenly the fugitives retired to the refuge they had chosen, and as sullenly did Mordred follow, hating those he had injured, hunting them to the death, and restrained only in his vindictive career by the clouded aspect of that dusky barrier, which he dared not brave.

By the side of the road, not far from the spot where in after days the piety of Athelstan founded the college and church of St. Buryan, there dwelt a holy hermit. In his poor cell one of the knights, whose wounds were mortal, laid down and departed from life. As the hermit knelt and prayed by his body, Mordred rode up. His face was pale as death, and was rendered still more ghastly by a blue livid wound, that traversed his whole forehead, and was lost amid his hair, matted and soaked with blood. He dismounted and entered the hut. The hermit and the dead man were its only tenants, save him. He looked upon the face of the corpse. It was the face of an early comrade of his own. The same blood ran in the veins of each of their mothers. He turned gloomily away and signed the sign of the cross, involuntarily, upon his breast. The hermit sighed, when he beheld the action. "Alas," said he to Mordred "thou hast in one day done more evil, than all thy ancestry have ever in their whole lives done of good. The crown of Arthur is upon thy brow, but the brand of Cain is there also. Go on, thou traitor to God and man." And Mordred smote him angrily with his gauntlet. "Go on," added the recluse, "thy course is wellnigh done. The shadow of a mighty one is brooding over thee. Go on, and die." And Mordred mounted his horse and urged it furiously forward. But the animal refused to obey the spur. The power of that dread spirit was before him. It had far more terrors for the charger than bit or steel. The avenging spectre would not give place to man's wrath. After a long and ineffectual struggle, the might of the unearthly prevailed. The ghastly chase was resumed, with the same dogged sullenness as before.

And now Mordred reached a lofty slope, from which, more clearly than he had hitherto been able to do, he could see his retiring enemies. They were already at a very considerable distance, upon that winding road which then led over the fertile tract of country called in Cornish "Lethowsow," or, in after-days, "the Lionesse." They

were so far in advance that he could only follow their
course by catching, at intervals, the gleaming of their arms.
Around him was that fair land, now so long lost and
forgotten, from the bosom of which men for ages had dug
mineral wealth, upon which were seen no fewer than one
hundred and forty stately churches, and whose beauty and
fruitfulness have been the theme of many a romantic lay.
Broken sunlight floated over its soft glades. It never
looked so grandly glorious as on that hour of its fate. As
Mordred pressed on, full of one thought alone, already in
imagination hemming in to slaughter, or driving into the
waves, his enemies, his attendants and followers began to
be sensible of a change in the atmosphere, of a something
oppressive and horrible, though he himself perceived it not.
Huge battlemented clouds, tinged with lurid red, hung over
the horizon. The air became sultry and choking. A
tremulous and wavy motion shook the ground at intervals.
A low sound, like distant thunder, moaned around. The
soldiers of his train drew closer together, awe-struck and
terrified. But Mordred heard only the evil voice of his own
passions. The war of the elements gave unmistakeable signs
of its awaking. But Mordred perceived it not.

At last, amid a silence that might be felt, so dreadful was
it, and so dull—that fearful shade, which had hitherto gone
before him, and restrained his madness, suddenly itself stopped.
It assumed a definite shape. It was the form of Merlin, the
Enchanter. But it was even more terrible than Merlin, for
it united the unearthly glare of the spectre with the grandeur
of the inspired man. Right in Mordred's path, face to face,
did the avenger stand. They remained for a few seconds,

motionless, frowning upon each other. Neither spake, save
with the eye. After those few seconds, the great wizard
raised his arm. Then there ensued a confused muttering, a
sound, as though the foundations of the great deep were
broken up. Soon the voice of the subterranean thunder
increased, and the firm soil beneath their feet began to welk
and wave, and fissures appeared upon the surface, and the
rock swelled like the throes of a labouring sea. With a wild
cry of agony, the band of pursuers became in turn the pur-
sued. They wheeled and rushed away in headlong flight.
But it was in vain. The earth, rent in a thousand fragments,
in the grasp of that earthquake, upheaved its surface
convulsively, gave one brief and conscious pause, and then,
at once, sank down for ever beneath the level of the
deep. In a moment, a continent was submerged, with all
its works of art, and piety, with all its living tribes, with
all its passions, and hopes, and fears. The soldiers of
Mordred were whirled away in the stream created by that
sudden gulf, which even now flows so violently over its prey
below. Last of all, Mordred remained, as it were fascinated
and paralyzed, gazing at the phantom with a look in which
horror struggled with hate, and which was stamped with
scorn and defiance to the end. That morning had dawned
upon as bright a scene as ever met the eye. At evening, there
was nought from what was then first termed the Land's-end,
to St. Martin's head, but a howling and boiling wilderness
of waves, bearing here and there upon its bosom a fragment
from the perished world beneath or a corse tossed upon the
billows, over which sea birds wheeled and screamed.

The remnant that was preserved reached in safety Cassiteris,

called afterwards Silura, and now Scilly.* There the wicked
ceased to trouble, and the weary were at rest. In their island
home, upon which still the sea encroaches daily, they dwelt
securely. From St. Martin's height, on their arrival, they
saw the catastrophe that overwhelmed their enemies, and,
dismounting, knelt upon the turf, and thanked God for their
deliverance. They never more sought the Britain of their
hope and fame. It would have been a changed and a
melancholy home for them. Arthur was in his tomb, at
Glastonbury. Guenever was dead. The Round Table was
broken and its best knights perished or dispersed. Their
work was done. In the Isles of Scilly, thus miraculously
severed from the main land, and, as it were set apart for
their sakes, they lived, and there they died. In after days
their children raised a stately religious house, at Tresco, over
their bones. But their memory gradually faded away and
was forgotten. Sometimes on a clear day there may be seen
the remains of walls or buildings under the sea. Sometimes
fishermen bring up relics of other times, and men wonder
at them and speculate upon their cause, and use. Strangers
make pilgrimages to Scilly, and marvel whether it ever
exceeded its present limits. But the account of its isolation
is remembered only as a confused dream; it is a mystery,
an old world tale; a fragment of which, like a portion of a
wreck, floats about, here and there, in the visions of the
past.

Such is the legend of the Lionesse.

---

* Another derivation of the word is from " Silya," the Cornish for
" conger," a fish plentiful and much valued here. See appendix.

CHAPTER IV.

SAINT MARY'S.

SAINT MARY'S* is the capital, as it were, of the islands; and Hugh Town is the capital of St. Mary's.

It is the most curious little place in the world. If Constantinople was originally called the city of the blind, from the mistake committed by its founders in choosing for it the worst site in the neighbourhood, Hugh Town has a fair prospect of being named the city of the drowned, for such will certainly be its end. It lies low on a neck of sand between two inlets or arms of the sea, St. Mary's pool, and Porcrasa bay,† which are about one hundred and fifty yards apart. The tide has several times broken over the narrow isthmus on which it stands, submerging the buildings that indeed scarcely are above its ordinary level. On Buzza

---

* So named from the patron saint of the abbey of Tavistock.
† Variously spelled, " Porth-cressa," or " Porth-crasou."

hill, to the south-east, can be traced the winding valley, from the old church to Hugh Town, where is seen, written in bold characters, the inevitable march of the waters. At a day, perhaps distant, perhaps very near, the garrison will form one islet, the high grounds of Buzza hill, and Peninnis, will become a second, leaving the main land still further shorn of its fair proportions by their loss. The ocean is an invader not easily baffled or repulsed. Within the memory of man it has covered two fields near the town, and has overflowed, and well-nigh swept away, the place itself. The inhabitants, meanwhile, sleep like Dutchmen under the shelter of their dykes. An Oriental never put greater faith in his kismet, or destiny, than a Scillonian in his immunity from drowning. They admit the probability of an inundation, but then, to engulf them, it requires so many concurrent visitations, such coincidences of tide, and wind, and moon, that they are content to take things as they are, and to wait for their prospective ducking with the most edifying and well-bred tranquillity. Just so did the people of old Port Royal, Jamaica, which may now be seen at low-water, offering a warning which no one heeds. Nature thus gives many a lesson to the world, but the world is a pupil that too often slights and neglects its master.

The people of Hugh Town are said to be very plain-spoken. The following anecdote is not a bad illustration of their talent in this line. When the chaplaincy was vacant, a clergyman came to see how the situation would suit him. He did duty at the church. After service, the sexton thus addressed him. "You won't do for the people here, Sir.

You reads too slow, and you keeps them in too long."
As for the general capacity of this part of England, I
heard a friend say, most irreverently, "that the more he
travelled in the west, the more was he convinced that the
wise men really came from the east."

And now, after this digression, I get again to Hugh Town.
I am not about to describe it, nor to write of Scilly in the
fashion of a local historian. That task has been performed,
accurately and ponderously enough, by no fewer than five
authors, Heath, Troutbeck, Borlase, Woodley, and North.
Their pages contain all that need be told, or learned, of the
physical and moral state of these islands. Finding, on my
arrival here, as a stranger, the want of some simple and
familiar guide to the traditions and the beauties of the Scilly
group, I have endeavoured to supply the void for the benefit
of others. I know nothing beyond what is on the surface, and
I seek to record only my first impressions of what I have
seen and heard. I will add the results of my observations
in a supplementary chapter, which may be perused or
skipped at pleasure.

Let me, *en passant*, enter my protest against the vast
amount of unnecessary learning brought to bear on the
names and annals of the islands. One writer, in particular,
is so enamoured of the antique, as to trace it in every phrase.*
A word is proved to be Greek, just as Fluellen proved the
similarity of Macedon and Monmouth, because there was a
river in both. An accidental coincidence in form, or in sound,

---

* "Pallestree." from "palæstra,"—place of strife. "Sallakee," from
"sullokáo," or "sule,"—prey, and "kéo,"—to dig. "Flagon," from
"phlégo,"—to burn. "Burrow," from "Pyramid!"

may exist in languages far removed from each other. Many
Saxon roots are found in Sanscrit, and there is no doubt that
Sanscrit is the foundation of Saxon, but because an English
word resembles Sanscrit, I do not conclude it to be neces-
sarily Indian. The ancients traded with these islands, but
they did not leave upon them the broad stamp of their
language and their memory.* On the contrary, I do not
believe that one Phœnician or Greek name can in reality be
traced. It is the national peculiarity of the English to affix
to the places they visit some appellation familiar, if not
grotesque. One historian objects to " Mount Flagon " as an
unmeaning designation, and tries to prove it Greek. The
next spot is " Brimstone hill." Another is " Taylor's
island." Beyond is the " Mare rock." Adjoining it is
" Crow sound." By a little ingenuity, I could make all
these Hebrew, but I prefer taking them for what they
really are.

Hugh Town, of which I have spoken twice before, is one
of the most wrong-headed little places in creation. Built as
I have described it, with one long, low, straggling street,
from which others branch off right and left, it presents no
very tempting appearance, until, at the upper end, there are
seen some good houses, and a very simple and handsome
church, towards the erection of which William the Fourth
gave £1000. It was finished by the munificence of the
Proprietor. The aspect of the lower town is sufficiently
miserable. On first walking through it I was struck, and

---

* " Porth, quasi portus," bay, is the only classical root which I have
found.

amused, with the word BANK, painted, in capital letters, upon a wretched hovel. Supposing the cottage to be the Exchange of St. Mary's, inhabited by the local Rothschild, I meditated a sketch of it. But, on inquiry, I found that the name was that of the situation, not of the house, which was built on rising ground. It was a warning to me, and to all other sight-seers, to ask before we decide. The lower town is terminated by a pier, begun by the Godolphin family, and finished by Mr. Augustus Smith. The shops are as good as might be expected, and contain a little of every thing, but the attendance is so dilatory, that we are reminded of the stupid waiter in Punch, who was represented as exclaiming hopelessly, on receiving a peremptory order from a customer in a hurry—" Oh, it's all very well to say look sharp." There is a market-place, which I mistook for a prison; and there is a real prison, so little formidable, that, during my stay, a man confined in it, walked out, and escaped, by getting on board a vessel in the pool. A clergyman, who is chaplain to the Proprietor, resides here, as well as a medical man of great ability; and there are some very respectable families in the place, which, like Leghorn, is full of odd costumes and odder faces from the foreign vessels that are constantly touching here. Its name is derived from the word " heugh " signifying a promontory in the sea. The inhabitants dress remarkably well, and the taste for finery is not confined to the adults. A friend of mine, the other day, met a little girl with a very smart black silk mantle. He said to her, " my dear, what a pretty polka you have got." " No sir," replied she, with a low curtsey, " it is not a polka, it is a visite."

At the north-eastern extremity of Hugh Town is " the
Garrison." It is about a mile and a quarter in circumference,
and rises, at its highest point, to somewhat more than one
hundred feet above the level of the sea. A broad road leads,
through the entrance gate, to Star Castle,* so called from
being built in the form of a star, or, as the Heralds would
emblazon it, an estoile of eight points. Following the path, the
opposite side of the peninsula is soon reached, through a
fragrant wilderness of furze, and heath, stocked with rabbits,
and with a fine herd of deer. Seats are placed at intervals for
those who love to linger amid scenes so fair. The charms
dwelling on this spot, and sanctifying it, are not those of
man's creating. The gloomy antique castle, the low dark
batteries, with their complement of six invalid artillerymen,
the dusky arch of the gate, have about them neither the spell
of beauty nor of romance. The red-cross banner of England,
that waves from yonder flagstaff, floats over an empire upon
which the sun never sets, but it has not flown, and will never
fly, above a brighter or a lovelier view. Beneath is the
noble bay, thronged with the shipping of all nations, which
have been driven hither by the easterly winds. A belt of
islands forms a frame to this characteristic picture of English
rule, the blue waves rolling against their rugged outlines,
and sparkling, in gay contrast, around their glittering white
sands. The air is heavy with perfume from the blossoming
furze. As you sit enjoying silently the prospect, a fawn
peeps at you from the brake, and after a moment's pause,

---

* It was erected in the reign of Elizabeth, whose initials, E.R. 1593,
are over the door, and was originally called " Stella Mariæ."

bounds timidly away. Nature is here perfect in her grandeur. If a trace of man intrude itself upon your solitude, it comes with an interruption as unwelcome, as it is abrupt. The hoarse bell of the watch-house startles you, while it rings out the hour. Over the glorious expanse of the sea a dismasted vessel comes lagging in, with its tale of sorrow and of pain.

The fortifications, as they are called, date from some century back. I hope they were erected in the time of George the Second. He professed to hate " boetry and bainting," and I could believe it, if the buildings on this hill were his handywork.

On leaving the Garrison, and crossing Porcrasa bay, you reach Buzza hill,* from the summit of which there is a charming view. A fine British barrow is to be seen here, two others having been destroyed to make room for a Spanish windmill, which occupies their site.

One word as to this queer exotic of brick and mortar. It is not generally known that a Spanish windmill is but a Lilliputian, compared with his English brother. The readers of Don Quixote are not aware that the knight, in attacking one, does not commit so monstrous an extravagance after all. Seen through the mist, with its revolving arms of white linen, it would present no very inapt resemblance to the white robed figure of a gigantic Moor. But the hero of La Mancha needs no apology. Genius has made him immortal, yet he is invested with a painful greatness, and

---

* Buzza, that is, Bosow hill, so called from a family of that name. Bant's Carn, Watts, Leg's, Banfield, Tol's, Thomas, have the same derivation.

the interest with which he inspires us is, to me, melancholy,
and sorrowful.   Byron has described it inimitably :—

> " Cervantes smiled Spain's chivalry away ;
>   A single jest demolished the right arm
> Of his own country. Never, since that day,
>   Has Spain had heroes. While romance could charm,
> The world gave ground before her bright array ;
>   And therefore have his volumes done such harm,
> That all their glory, as a composition,
>   Was dearly purchased by his land's perdition.
>   *   *   *   *
> Of all books 'tis the saddest,—not less sad
>   Because it makes us smile !''

What a proof have we here of the spell exercised by genius
over time and space.   We are on a lone hill, surrounded,
to all human seeming, by rocks and waves.   In a moment,
in a point of time, the mind journeys on its pilgrimage to the
Sierra Morena, and brings the spirit of old Saavedra to
commune with it above this silent and solitary carn.   The
roguish horse-dealer boasting to Gil Blas of his honesty,
protested that it was his " lado mas flaco " his weakest side.
Truly, if a man has in his nature a particle of romance, it
is sure to find him out.   It discovers for him kindred that
he dreamed not of, and shows him his unguarded point, " his
own infirmity," even when he expects it least.

Advancing to the south, you pass the Dutchman's carn,
and reach Peninnis head.*   The rocks here are of extra-
ordinary beauty.   To an artist, probably, they have no rival
anywhere in the island.   They present every variety of form,
from the broad massy square, resembling the keep of a
Norman hold, to the tall tooth-rock, and the pulpit, with its

---

* " Pen-ynys,"—head of the islands.

vast canopy of stone. The whole coast is striking, and even sublime. Art, too, is not wanting, in aid of its effect. For this spot, so full of natural grandeur, is pitched upon by antiquaries for the scene of one of their bitterest contentions. Here, in fact, are the celebrated rock basins. What are they? Are they accidental formations, or artificial? Are they cisterns, like those of the ancient Mexicans, or are they Druidical remains? Are they for lay purposes, or for holy uses? Troutbeck and Borlase attribute them to the Druids. Davies Gilbert calls them " supposed relics." North considers them the work of chance. I should say that there would not be a doubt about the matter, to any one but an antiquary, who is a misty kind of animal, tarnishing and obscuring all upon which he lays his touch. " Here," quoth Monkbarns, waxing eloquent as he described to his guest the imaginary Roman camp, " here was the Prætorian gate." " Prætorian here, Prætorian there," replied Edie Ochiltree, " I mind weel the bigging o't!" So is it with the Rock basins. The rain has evidently decomposed the granite, and formed, in the course of ages, these rounded cells, christened so loftily! At all events, common sense must settle the question, for history is mute, unless we can hope for such a solution as was once proposed by my old master, Bishop Butler, for a similar case. Shrewsbury school rejoiced in an interminable Chancery suit, which could only be settled by the evidence of a certain Abbot, who died three hundred years ago; and the Bishop suggested that he should be summoned accordingly, and either examined, or pronounced contumacious, and so the matter would be finally arranged.

Every island in the world, I believe, has its peculiar

" Piper's hole." There is one here, which is said to communicate with its grander sister at Tresco, so that a dog,
entering one, passed out at the other. To be sure, they point
different ways, but it is hardly fair to mar a tale of mystery
by an objection so commonplace. Let us rather listen, and
walk on, gazing on the " great south," as it lies before us,—

" darkly, deeply, beautifully, blue,"

while we enjoy the majesty of these rugged piles around,
which Time's hand has hallowed, and endowed with a power
such as he only can bestow. Beyond them the eye rests on
nothing but the Infinite of sky and sea, and upon that distance
brooding over dim space, which is in itself sublime, like the
Spirit of God, moving upon the face of the waters.

After turning the extreme point of the island, you reach
an irregular path, which leads you to Old Town. It lies at
the head of the little bay, on one side of which is the small
deserted Church, and on the other a large cluster of houses.
This was the ancient capital of St. Mary's.* Its aspect is
that of sadness and decay. In such a situation Ruin is a fit
dweller. One of the aged mariners, inhabiting that grey
group of dwellings, might well say with Tennyson,—

> " And no more shall we roam,
> O'er the loud hoar foam.
> From our melancholy home,
> On the limits of the brine,
> From the little isle of Hesperus,
> Beside the day's decline."

A respectable looking man touched his hat civilly to me, as
I leaned upon the stile. I asked him to whom the Castle,
now in ruins, had belonged.

---

* In perfect keeping with it is an ancient kist-vaen, built into the corner
of an outhouse, near the path.

"I am sure I can't tell you, sir," was the reply of the worthy Scillonian, "but it was destroyed by Oliver Cromwell."

Here, as afterwards at Bryher and elsewhere, I was met by the ghost of the stern old Protector. The fortress, a few stones of which are seen upon the rocky mound, was smitten by an arm more terrible than even his, by a Power " whose hand is a hand of iron, and its blow is death." It has known no worse foe than Time. It was mouldering already in the days of Leland, when the family of the Kingkiller bore the name of Williams, and ere his Welch great grandfather had assumed that of Cromwell, in honour of his patron, the Earl of Essex. Its stones were quietly removed in the time of Elizabeth, principally to build Star Castle. But even while we know this, we cannot shake off the spell of mind. The Druid is still the ruler of these carns and cromlechs. The spirit of old Oliver comes to brood wherever death has been, grim, ghostly, impalpable, a principle, rather than a real corporeal existence, seated always amid destruction, like Arimanes on his throne.

When I got back to my lodgings, my landlady's servant met me, with the following questions.

"Pray, sir, would you like a chicken for dinner?"

"By all means, if you please."

"Pray, sir, would you like it roasted brown *on both sides?*"

Beyond Old Town there rises abruptly from the sea a bold shelf of rocks, called Tolmen, or Tollman head. Tradition says that it was so named from a tax, or toll, being imposed upon all persons who landed there. This custom, and an incident connected with it, form the subject of the following tale.

CHAPTER V.

TOLL-MAN HEAD, A LEGEND OF OLD TOWN.

RICHARD, Earl of Cornwall, was a powerful prince, surpassing in wealth and resources many sovereigns of his day. The revenue he derived from his Cornish mines was prodigious. He seated a large colony of Jewish merchants at Marazion, called, differently, by the name of "Margha-Zion,"* market of the Mount, meaning that of St. Michael; or "Mara-Zion," bitter Zion, in allusion to the abject state of God's fallen people; or Market Jew. By granting great privileges to the sons of Israel, and by sternly protecting them from wrong, he sagaciously turned to his own profit their talents for business. Under their direction, Marazion, or Market Jew, became a great place of export for those ores, which, from time immemorial, have rendered Cornwall so celebrated. The mineral trade of England seemed to be centred in Mount's-bay, where, centuries before, the galleys of the Phœnicians had come to

---

* Or, according to Carew, "Margha-diou,"—Thursday market, which is a mistake, the market being held on Saturday.—*Carew's Survey of Cornwall*, 1602-1669.

deal, by barter, with the rude natives. The monks of St. Michael's Mount cursed the unholy lust of gain which drew together, beneath the very shadow of their blessed walls, and close to the great cross of Edward the Confessor, and under the chapel on the rock, these detested strangers. The flourishing town of Marazion swarmed with their well known features. Their sordid gabardines, and yellow caps, were exchanged for robes better befitting their worldly circumstances. Their wives and daughters bore, even in public, dresses of Eastern fabric, and the edges of their manches, and of their hoods, were trimmed with costly miniver. They gave back, with interest, the scorn of the monks. And they were, in turn, an abomination to the men of God, though these last marvelled at the beauty of some of those maids of Judah, for, sooth to say, many of the damsels were very fair to look upon.

It was principally from this source that Earl Richard raised that wealth which enabled him to purchase from the venal electors the dignity of King of the Romans, and entitled him to aspire to the imperial diadem. It was then, and from such hopes as these, that he assumed, among his armorial bearings, those bezants, or byzantines, in memory of which so many gentlemen of Cornwall bore, and still bear, the bezant on their shields. But, while from motives of interest, or of wise policy, thus protecting an important branch of commerce, the Earl was not a partial ruler. He suffered no subordinate tyranny. He would not allow the Jews to be oppressed nor wronged, neither would he permit them to oppress nor to wrong others. He upheld all classes of his subjects in their just rights. He supported, in all their

privileges, the religious orders. He preserved all their im-
munities untouched and inviolate. Yet this fact did not
make him popular with the Church, as it might be supposed
to do. The word franc-maçonero, or freemason, in Spain,
under the reign of Ferdinand the beloved, was not a more
deadly charge than was that of favourer of the Jews, in the
days of which I write.* Such was then the feeling towards
the once chosen people. Men whispered among each other
that the gold in Earl Richard's coffers would ·be found
leaves or ashes, since it was the produce of those circumcised
dogs, and they shook their heads, and made the holy sign,
and prophecied evil things of the stout Earl.

In another part of his broad lands, the Prince was equally
disliked, though from a different cause. The great group
of Scilly was not then what it is now,—a vast body of little
more than rocks,—but consisted of several large islands,
the centre of an important traffic, filled with a numerous
and flourishing population, and supporting many religious
establishments. St. Martin's, Tresco, Bryher, Samson's, and
all the adjacent places, then formed one chief main land,
under the rich Abbey of Tresco, and were held of it, for the
most part, by bridle and spear, as the fief of a bold Baron of
the Norman house of Barentin. St. Mary's was likewise far
more extensive than at present. It had wealthy houses also
at Old Town, and Friar's Carn, and Holy Vale. The monks
and nuns monopolised all the sources of profit, and though
their rule was neither unfair nor heavy, yet it generally

---

* I remember once being told that a Spanish girl turned upon an
English officer with horror, and spat in her disgust upon the ground,
on being informed by him that our Saviour was a Jew.

happens that clerical landlords, from some reason or other, are unpopular; and so it was with the brotherhoods and sisterhoods of St. Mary's. They took no more than their due, though they took their due, even from the hard-working fishermen. The shaven crowns waxed sadly unpopular. But Earl Richard supported them in their sway, and refused to listen to the charges brought against them. There was a report that he failed continually in all his enterprises, how well planned soever they might be, and that, without giving up his lucrative patronage of the Jews, he wished to propitiate the favour of heaven by showing countenance to its servants. Certain it is, however, that all his schemes miscarried, but, in an equal ratio to their want of success, his kindness to the monastic orders increased. He upheld them with a high hand in all their charters and grants. So that it soon became as dangerous to wag a finger against a frock or a cowl, as against the Earl himself. The Earls of Cornwall had been a fierce and fiery race, loving war and wassail, as did most of the princes of the house of Plantagenet, the most gallant and magnificent dynasty that ever filled a throne. But in that age it was shrewdly remarked, that, in proportion to the excesses of his life, was a Norman noble's penitence on his death bed; and this penitence was usually shown in substantial gifts to the Church, and not unfrequently by assuming her priestly robes, ere the sinner passed away. It was the same feeling that, in Italy, makes a Brigand consider himself sure of Paradise, if, after a life of murders, he is lucky enough to go to the scaffold, with a priest murmuring absolution in his ear. Now the heirs of a great house had no objection to the death bed

repentance, but were apt to oppose very bitterly the cession
of worldly substance that, somehow or other, was made to
form an indispensable condition of the bargain for heaven.
After this fashion, the Earls of Cornwall had been profuse
in penitence.   Like old Hugh de Mortimer, as related in
Dugdale, they had bought remission at other people's expense,
and grievous were the heart-burnings caused by their pious
generosity.   Earl Reginald, son of Henry the First, had
bestowed upon St. Nicholas of Iniscaw, or Trescaw, and upon
the shrines of St. Mary, St. Kumon, and St. Warna, and had
confirmed to them in fee, every wreck in the islands, "except
whale and a whole ship."   Edmund, the last Earl, heaped
wealth and power upon the Church.   The brethren were the
virtual lords of the islands, and did not bear themselves very
meekly in the discharge of their functions.   At the time of
my tale, they were somewhat haughtier and more peremptory
than usual.   As a counterpoise to his support of the Jews
elsewhere, Earl Richard went to the contrary extreme at
Scilly.   He abetted the good fathers in their vindication of
their rights ; and not only suffered no man to do them wrong,
but, it was whispered, allowed them, on the contrary, to do
wrong to others, by stretching the law in their favour to the
utmost.   The Prior of Trescaw frequently exhorted his
flock against covetousness, and was very fond of enlarging
on the text " He reproved even kings for their sakes," and
of applying these words to the defence of their rights by
Earl Richard.   The Sire de Barentin, a shrewd and stout
old warrior, twirled his grey moustache, and said nothing,
though there was a curious and humorous expression in his
eye, which the worthy Prior did not care to fathom.   But

the common people, with bated breath, murmured to each
other, as they went home, that, of the two parties which their
Lord was accused of encouraging too much, they would
rather have the Jew than the Priest. It was easy, they said,
to spy the cloven foot, and to be on your guard against it,
but the wisdom of the great serpent himself could never get
to the bottom of a Monk's hood.

Now among the claims of the good Fathers, there was one
that gave especial dissatisfaction, even more than the exclusive
right to wrecks. This was a somewhat onerous poll-tax,
imposed indiscriminately on every person landing on the
island. The principal port was then, as it is now, called Old
Town, but it was at that time in a state far different from its
present aspect of ruin. Standing in Old Town bay, and
facing the sea, you beheld, to the right, a stately church
and monastic pile. In front, on the left hand, was a massy
landing-place, and pier, the ruins of which are still visible;
and, above, towered the noble castle of the Earls of Cornwall, while the whole circuit of the shore was lined with
houses, and edifices connected with trade. The point,
however, to which my legend principally refers, was a small
cluster of buildings a little in advance, to the left. It
consisted of an humble shrine or chapel, and a simple kind
of guard-house, across the front of which was stretched an
iron chain, forming a barrier before a broad flight of steps,
that led upwards from the quay, and gave access to the
island. It was by this way that strangers first approached
land. This projection was called Tolman or Toll-man point,
the name being derived from a toll levied by the Monks on
every person, without distinction, who set his foot on the

shore. They held this power by a grant from a former Earl,
confirmed to them by Earl Richard. The revenue they
derived from it was not inconsiderable, and was rigidly ex-
acted; nor was there any one of their claims which gave
such dire offence. It was not only said to be a Pagan
custom (in support of which assertion people showed a huge
rock on the spot, called Tolmen or, " hole-stone," and
affirmed that it was an object of Druidical adoration, to
which they made every worshipper pay toll), but it pressed
most unjustly upon the very poorest class, for every fisherman
who left the island, though only for a few hours, to gain a
little support for his family, was compelled to give his mite, in
the way of tribute, on his return. Nay, even holy Palmers
from the East, who were always elsewhere considered
exempt from tax or charge, were forced to render the dues,
ere they were permitted to proceed. This was said to be an
infraction of the charter, and a clear violation of that most
pious and equitable statute, that no priest nor pilgrim ought
ever, under any circumstances, to *pay* any thing, the duty of
the good men being solely to *receive;* but the monks, strong
in the buckler of the faith, and of Earl Richard, spoiled
not only the Egyptians, but their own order, most pitilessly.
Complaints were made, long and loudly, to the Earl, who
promised redress, and with some intention of granting it,
for he was in sad want of a subsidy, and these allegations,
if proved, would authorise him to exact a pretty heavy
benevolence from the transgressors, or raise a goodly sum,
by way of bounty, on their lands.

It was a sunny evening in May when a small company of
pilgrims was seen on the deck of a vessel, that neared the

harbour of Old Town, with a favourable wind. They bore down directly to the foot of the steps at Toll-man point, which, as it was then high-water, they reached without difficulty. On coming alongside the broad stones that formed a base to the stairs, they sprang ashore, and began to ascend. At their head was one apparently of higher rank, or of superior sanctity, for he walked alone. His face was partly buried in his large cloak, and partly concealed beneath his wide-brimmed hat, the deep flaps of which, hanging down, were often employed to hide the features. He passed on, neither speaking, nor apparently heeding any thing, until he reached the heavy chain, which was drawn across the way. Laying his hand upon it, he found that it was fastened with a padlock. As one of the brothers was sitting in the toll-house, reading, as it seemed, his book of prayers, the Pilgrim, after several vain attempts to undo the chain, called to him, in a firm but courteous voice, to unfasten it, and give him passage.

It chanced that the person thus addressed was the Prior, who, having sent the occupant of the place on an errand, had, during his absence, taken his post. Angry at being thus interrupted, and scarcely seeing who it was that spoke, he bade the new comers wait awhile, and resumed his studies. The Pilgrim, however, seemed in no mood to do as he was told. "How now, Sir Priest," replied he, "you are malapert, forsooth. Open as I bid you, and let us pass. There is no toll levied on such as we."

The tone in which he spoke was stern and sharp, but the Prior was an old man, hard of hearing, cold and unbending in his disposition, and too much accustomed to this kind of

complaint to pay attention to it. He glanced slightly at
the group, but looked down again, and made no reply.
He was not, however, long suffered to remain in peace.
Laying his hand upon the chain, the Pilgrim vaulted over,
and stood before the Prior's seat, his form erect, his eyes
flashing fire, and his whole figure convulsed with passion.
A prudent man would have let him go unchallenged, but
the Prior was spoiled by the habits of unquestioned power,
which Ecclesiastics of that day assumed over every rank
and class. He was, besides, a proud resolute man, who had
been a soldier in his youth, and had ridden through a stricken
field. His apathy was gone at once. Rising up, with
considerable dignity, and drawing to its full height his spare
and ascetic form, he laid his hand upon the Pilgrim's breast,
and bade him stand back. It was an evil chance that he did
so. His hand had scarcely touched the Palmer's chest, ere
the latter flung his cloak aside, raised his mailed arm,
and smote the old man rudely upon the head. "Dog of a
Priest, thou cowled robber," he cried, in a voice of thunder,
"take that, as a memento of Richard Plantagenet." And
the Prior sank at his feet, bathed in blood, and over him
stood Earl Richard, looking darkly down upon him as he
lay.

They raised the old man, and tried to stanch the gore that
welled from his temples, but in vain. The blow was given by
a hand that seldom struck twice. He opened his eyes, and
looked upon the Earl, whose hot fit was already succeeded
by sorrow and remorse. Richard took the Prior's hand, and
spoke to him kindly, but the sufferer was already almost
beyond the reach of human blame or praise. He glanced at

the Prince, and then at the castle that frowned above them. The spirit of prophecy, which is said to visit the dying, seemed to tremble on his lips. He whispered, rather than said, " Lord Earl, that blow has stricken both thy house, and thee." And word he spake never more.

The prediction was fulfilled. Earl Richard made all the amends in his power. He abolished the toll, and gave to the brethren, in exchange, great largesses, far surpassing in value what he had resumed. On the spot that had witnessed his crime he founded a chantry, where masses were daily said for the soul of the murdered man. But from that hour the Earl's affairs declined. He wasted his wealth in unprofitable enterprises, and, finally, went down to the grave, a broken, moody, miserable man.

Nor did the curse fail of its accomplishment on the spot. It never prospered again. The sea gradually encroached upon the land, and swallowed up field after field of fruitful ground. The stately church was injured by a storm, and was rebuilt in diminished size and beauty. The castle fell to ruin, why and wherefore no one could tell. Storms of thunder and lightning, so uncommon in Scilly, occurred constantly. Sailors and traders began to shun the place, and believed it haunted by the ghost of the dead Prior, which, it was said, was often seen at Toll-man head, exacting tribute from a spectral figure, at the head of an equally unsubstantial train. At last the usual effects of such rumours followed. Merchants first landed in a pleasant bay near at hand called Porcrasa, and then discovered that in St. Mary's pool beyond there was a safer and surer anchorage. Fishermen took thither their produce for sale. So a town was formed by

degrees, and on the hill above, a fort dedicated to the Virgin,
and called " Stella Mariæ," or the " Star of Mary" was
afterwards built.

Thus there came down upon the Old Town gloom, and
desolation, and decay. The ancient Druids who worshipped
there, seem to overshadow it still with their dim phantom
presence. The blackness of the churchman's malediction is
still resting there. The Druid goddess, Onvana, the sea,
gains upon it daily, and Taranis, the Thunderer, is often
heard. It seems abandoned to gloomy influences, and, seen
on a darksome day, is a place whose melancholy is not
soon shaken off. At no distant period it will be buried
beneath the ocean, which will roll silently over all that
remains of its former greatness, and leave only a few
sibylline leaves, as records of its past history, with the
memory of " the old man's curse."

CHAPTER VI.

SAINT MARY'S. No. 2.

WENT to-day on a hunt for antiquities; and not only for antiquities, but for the natural beauties among which the relics of the past repose. Perhaps there does not exist a combination of what is stern and sublime, in God's works and in the creations of man, more perfect than the objects of my pilgrimage to-day. My guide was a lady, whose knowledge of all that is interesting in these islands, and whose keen appreciation of their romantic grandeur, is as charming as it is unrivalled.

In the outskirts of Hugh Town, as elsewhere, you are struck by a peculiarity in the roofs. Wherever they are formed of straw, they are not made, after the usual fashion, with large eaves, but are fastened down, bodily, by twisted bands, which are secured firmly to pegs in the wall. This precaution is taken to prevent the thatch from being blown off by the wind. Every house has a porch with a side door, to break the force of the gales, which, if admitted in front, would be irresistible. Nearly all the windows, also, are screwed down, opening only a little at the top. The skeleton which, it is said, exists in every cupboard, is here the visitation of periodical storms, of a violence hardly to be described. Yet the Scillonian winter is not a winter, after all, frosty, but kindly, crowned with holly, and redolent of good cheer, but, like the Indian summer in Canada, an intruder into a season not his own. The gales, indeed, blow heavily at Christmas, but the true scourge of Scilly is the east wind of March and April. This year it has raged for nearly three months, with a deadly effect hardly to be described. Still it is curious how limited is its range. Vessels from the Atlantic have had a strong westerly breeze, until they came close to land. Perhaps these opposing currents may account for the singular set of the stream round these rocks. It runs in a complete circle; so that a vessel, which was wrecked here some time ago, was carried round the islands for three days, and was then by chance, only, thrown upon a bank of sand.*

Ascending Buzza, or Bosow hill, and visiting the site of the one remaining barrow, or burrow,† we struck across the

---

* I may as well here mention another trait of Scillonian life. Adam Smith proved the existence of commerce, in the way of barter, by the example in the Iliad, where a suit of brass armour was valued against a number of oxen. I can produce a more modern instance from my own experience. As there is here no great demand for meat, so the supply is limited and unvaried. To obtain a change of diet, being unable to buy, I was very glad to exchange a piece of beef for a calf's head.

† Troutbeck says that this word is derived from the Saxon "bysigean," to bury.

country, by a path on the top of a wall, as is customary in Cornwall. Keeping to the south-east, we soon reached Old Town, and looked at the ancient kist-vaen, now built into the corner of a stable, and at Toll-man head, and examined a rock basin or two, of which I can only repeat my opinion that they are natural. We then descended to the little bay, the name of which, Porth Minich, or Porth Menich, is believed to be a corruption of Porth Monach,* especially as the adjoining carn is called Church Ledge. Crossing the fields that bound it, we came in sight of a wide down, yellow with golden furze, and studded with carns, and barrows, and huge grey stones. Before us, on the right, high over the sea, was the Giant's Castle, and to it we bent our steps. The ground rises continually, and is covered with a kind of mossy turf, not level, nor uniform, but worn in channels, and broken with innumerable rocks.†

The fâde compliment paid by the Frenchman to his mistress, when seated on a green, "Madame, l'uni-verd (l'univers) est à vos pieds," would by no means be applicable here.

The Giant's Castle is well worth a visit. It is probably a Danish stronghold, and consists of three circles of intrenchments, the inner one being the citadel. Round a ledge of rock, to the right, is a fine logan, or logging, stone. I mounted to the top, while my lady companion rocked it to and fro. We proceeded along the shelf of the cliff, till we faced the great ocean, then tumbling and rolling wildly in, and breaking in thunder upon the beach below. There was nothing between

---

* Monachorum, or monks.

† The irregularity was caused by the former habit of cutting turf, now happily prohibited.

us and Newfoundland, save the spirit of the vasty deep, and
the power of Him who stilleth the raging of the waves.
A large Indiaman, bringing the news of the loss of the
Birkenhead stream frigate, at the Cape, with nearly five
hundred souls, went slowly by, with sails close reefed,
pitching heavily. Yet in this stormy spot, a human being
once found refuge from pursuit. On the other side of the
promontory is a cave called Tom Butt's bed, from a boy of
that name, who, to escape at once impressment, and a cruel
master, hid himself here. He was discovered by some boys,
through whose aid he was supplied with food, and finally
got on board a ship, and found safety in flight.

Below the Castle is Porthhellick bay. The whole of the
open ground around is called Sallakee down. In 1840 a
shipwreck occurred here, under circumstances probably
unparallelled. A French vessel, from Dunkerque, was upset,
and three men were kept alive in her hold, and so preserved.
The ship drifted on the sands, and the voyagers were rescued
by the aid of a fisherman, who happened to be there. My
companion saw the vessel. She told me that the first thing
done by the poor Frenchmen, on reaching land, was to fall
down upon their knees, and return thanks to God. At the
corner of the bay is shown, truly or falsely, the grave in which,
for a time, was interred the famous Sir Cloudesley Shovel.
The account of his wreck is given in North. An air of romance
has been thrown over his fate by the circumstances said to
have preceded it. A sailor on board the flag ship warned the
Admiral that he was sailing direct for the rocks of Scilly.
The man, according to one account, was charged with
endeavouring to excite a mutiny and was hung. According

to another version, he was punished, and by a sort of poetical justice, was the only person saved. He floated to a rock beyond, called the Hellweathers and was got off next day. The body of Sir Cloudesley was identified, though naked, by a diamond ring which he always wore. He was interred in the sand, but taken up again, and buried in Westminster Abbey. Tradition says that the grass never grew again upon his unblest grave. About two thousand persons perished at the same time, among whom were his step-son Sir John Narborough, and Mr. Henry Trelawny, son of Bishop Trelawny, one of those committed to the Tower by King James the Second, and of whom the memory is preserved by the old Cornish verse,—

> " And shall they slay Tre, Pol, and Pen,
> And shall Trelawny die ?
> Then forty thousand Cornish men
> Shall know the reason why."

There is a large pond of fresh water near the cove, and several Druidical circles and barrows about it. As at Stonehenge, the neighbourhood of these circles seems to have been a favourite spot for interment. Many of these burying places have been opened, but I believe nothing has been found but black, greasy, strongly smelling earth. Keeping parallel to the sea, and crossing the downs, we arrived at what is called the Druid's chair. The seat faces due east, and the Arch-Druid is said to have sate in it, to observe the rising of the sun. We must leave the truth of this story to internal evidence, for we can neither affirm nor contradict it. It is certainly a comfortable resting-place, but scarcely an artificial one, for there are many just as good, in different parts of the islands, and facing in all directions. Above it is a circle, with barrows innumerable. I do not give the local designations of the many rocks and carns, for they would convey no definite meaning to the reader, and he would find the list as tiresome on paper, as the reality is picturesque and sublime.

This Druid priesthood was a remarkable race. They taught to the commom people a debased Polytheism, but while to the vulgar they told of Taranis, the thunderer, and Hesus, the god of war, and Belus, the sun, and Onvana, the ruler of the waves, their own creed, as is supposed to have been the case with the Egyptian initiated, was widely different. The Pantheon of the Priest had but one God, God the Invisible!

> " For there the Druid never knelt before
> His own device, to worship and adore,
> Nor blindly deemed that human art could throne
> A God's bright presence in a form of stone.
> Oh no! he turned his philosophic eye
> To the broad ocean, and the pathless sky,
> And from the mountain, and the torrent. caught
> That deep and stern sublimity of thought,
> That loves to gaze on nature's shrine, and see,
> Above, around, pervading Deity." *

Like the Saga, the faith of the Druid was the creation of the land from which he sprung. Grand, solitary, savage, it came home to the feelings, in such scenes as these. Its rude sublimity impressed itself upon nature, and a thousand years have passed over, but not eradicated it. The Culdee has not left even the shadow of his worship. The Saxon Gods are forgotten. Thor, and Odin, and Zernebock, do not exist in a memory or a fragment; but, through the length and breadth

---

* The Druids : Cambridge prize poem, by J. S. Brockhurst.

of the land, the Druid and his hypœthra, his rock temples, that bare their bosoms to heaven, survive, and seem immortal. There is nothing mean, nor little, nor common, in that which defies time. Sit in the Druid's chair, and look, over that great ocean, at the sun. So, perchance, did the Priest, for whose worship those rings of stone, and that channel to carry off the blood of the victim, were made, perhaps, twenty centuries ago. The mind that in spite of error, stamped its impress upon such a space of time as that, was a master mind, a mind of such an order as, in Christendom, forms an apostle or a martyr, and, in a cause of beautiful deceit, a Mahomet or a Numa.

We returned slowly over the down, pausing at times to observe carns and tumuli. Through a narrow lane, which passes a farm-house boasting the name of London, we gained an excellent road, that conducts the traveller to Hugh Town. On the right of the highway is a mass of rocks called Carnefriars, which is evidently a corruption of Carn-Friars, or Carn-Prior. We have here, as in the neighbouring appellation of Holy Vale, a proof of the existence of several religious communities. There is scarcely any tradition to preserve the tale of their existence. Perhaps some Friar John, or Friar Roger, performed there exploits worthy of Chaucer's clerks. Perhaps some Anchorite dwelt in the clefts of the rocks, or peradventure the solitude was hallowed by the abode of many such, better than those whom Boccaccio has immortalized, and, when they shuffled off their mortal coil,

> " The monks of St. Nicholas said 'twas ridiculous
> Not to suppose every one was a Saint."

We retraced our steps to Hugh Town. The Spanish
windmill on Buzza hill gazed down curiously upon us, at
the end of the long vista, formed by our road. This windmill
was erected by the son of a person who had been many years
in our Commissariat, in Spain. I remember once in Italy
seeing Bolsena, mouldering, it was quaintly said, over
Volsinium. The mill, already in appearance old, is going
to decay over the dust of the ancient Lords of the soil. It
stands upon the funeral barrows of those, our departed
ancestors, who at autumn fall bought the hallowed fire from
the same Druids, in whose sacred chair I had, perhaps, sate
to-day. A little below it, to the right, was the tower of the
church, beautiful in its simplicity. The mariner from Spain,
whose vessel is wind-bound in the harbour, looks upon the
memorial of his country, and remembers the " va con Dios"
that cheered him as he left his home. The Protestant sees
in the fabric, rising to our eyes from the hillside, a bond of
union, and a memento of his common Christendom, a sign
of that faith which is for the universe and for eternity;

> " A shrine more pure than ever Pagan trod,
>   The Christian's temple, to the Christian's God."

CHAPTER VII.

SAINT MARY'S. No. 3.

O-DAY I finished my survey of St. Mary's Isle, which, indeed deserves to be visited, not in the spirit of those who "peep and botanize," but with all the feeling of high art, and with a keen appreciation of its lights and shadows. I started from Hugh Town in the afternoon, and followed the path to the left, winding round Permellin, or Porthmellin, bay.

On the hill above us are seen some ruins, called Harry's walls.* They are all that remain of what was intended to be a fortress, in the reign of Henry the Eighth, but it was never finished. Such was the excellence of the cement used in its construction, that it defies man's efforts to remove it; and there it stands, Mr. Barry, a lesson to you, and to the other architects of this enlightened age. Had I asked an old man, who was working near the spot, the history of those grey stones, if he had not, as most probably he would have done, said something after the fashion of the Spaniard or the Italian, *chi sa*, or *quien sabe*, I should have been referred to the omnipresent destroyer, Oliver Cromwell, so I held

---

* Near them is a fine Menhir.

my peace. What a singular trait in the idiosyncrasy of this
people is their total want of curiosity about the past,* their
general absence of tradition and of storied memories ! Races
and generations have ruled here, and have passed away.
A rock temple beneath the sky is the tomb of a departed
priesthood; yonder curtain and bastion tell a tale of the
grim sovereign at whose bidding they arose, and who
probably flung down an altar or a monastery to furnish
materials for them ; the site of Tresco Abbey speaks of its
ancient faith ; the lonely tower on the hillside beyond is a
memorial of the Puritans, and was itself erected from the
fragments of a castle of the Plantagenets. At all this you
must guess, since you will look in vain for any aid to be
found from the natives, or on the spot. The round towers
of Ireland are not a greater puzzle to its Celts than are
the relics of other days to their kindred here. Antiquity
has, perhaps, left a treasure under their feet, but what do
they care ? The fate of all the argosies ever stranded on
their shores is nothing, in their eyes, to a lucky salvage,—
like that of the West Indiaman, wrecked on the rocks of
Samson, this spring. As Körner says, it is,—

> " Überall Leben,
> Überall streben,
> Überall sonnenschein."

Above Permellin bay is a cluster of comfortable houses,
and a good road is in process of formation. Indeed, the

---

* This is a strong proof of a complete change of race. A tribe
or family always preserves it own records, but neglects those of its
predecessors. So the ruined cities of South America, in their vastness,
are to us a sealed book. Their builders are gone, and those that came
after them recked not of them.

highways are marvellously perfect. Nor, in them are comfort and convenience disregarded. They have a gravelled footpath, bordered with stone, and, at intervals, many a handsome seat, on which an anagram, with the date, 1847, informs you to whose munificence, and kind superintendence, you are indebted for this accommodation.

After visiting Carn Morval, from whence is a magnificent view of the pool, there is an ascent to the telegraph, which rises two hundred and ten feet above the level of the sea. Near it again is a fine menhir, or upright stone, probably an object of Druidical worship. There is also an opened barrow, or tomb, of great extent, and very perfect. The Catholics do not seem here, as in Brittany, to have added crosses to these idols, and so to have appropriated them to their own faith. In the course of my walk I saw another of these shapeless rocks, and barrows almost numberless, some being in remarkably fine preservation. There is a farm also, called Normandy, so named, perhaps, by some emigrant from old Neustria, as our countrymen in Australia bear with them the remembrance of their native homes. We passed Inisidgen point, Sandy bar, the Crow rock, and Helveor, which are so many points of beauty, each with its peculiar features, redeeming it from monotony, and giving to it its own wild stamp and impress. After visiting the neighbourhood of Mount Todden, and so completing the circuit of the island, we turned inland. We remarked many farm-houses, evidently in a most prosperous state, and many comfortable cottages. The crops were extremely good, the principal one, being here, as elsewhere, the early potato. If you want to judge of the character of a landlord, go and look at the condition of his farm-houses, and of his peasantry.

On a large open space, called the Green, there was a considerable number of young people, of both sexes, collected, the men playing at cricket, and the women and children in groups watching them. Being Easter Tuesday, I find that to-day an annual fair or feast is held in this place, and is, I should think, a relic of some custom handed down from other times. The locality too is singular, for the Green is just above *Holy Vale*, and the celebration was, probably, in some way connected with the ecclesiastics, and under their patronage, and was meant to be an indulgence after the mortifications of Lent.

From the crest of the descent to Holy Vale, called May-pole hill, the view is very beautiful. The Pulpit rock and the old church are in the distance. Around you lie cultivated fields, interspersed with the sweetest wilderness of flowering gorse and heather that you ever had the good fortune to see. Hugh Town and its " castled crags " stand out in bold relief. Above your head, a peregrine falcon is wheeling with long majestic swoops. And at your feet reposes in its picturesque groves, here full of rare and strange loveliness, though no longer consecrated by affection or by piety, the little oasis of Holy Vale.

Lacordaire, the famous Roman Catholic preacher, has said, very finely, that while human institutions fade away and are forgotten, with their founders, there seems a spell and a sacredness in the mere name of God that all men confess and honour. Look at the poets. Ask five men out of ten in the world who Homer was, and they will stare at you in

silent surprise. How many nations did the philosophy of
Plato rule or convert? How much do people of the present
day, or of many a one that is past, care about Socrates? Did
Demosthenes found a sect, or do men bow at the name of
Cicero? Look on the other hand at the contrast shown by
religion, even when false. Look at the religious books, even
of Heathenesse. What makes " the Kings," the " Vedas,"
the law of Confucius, the " Koran," immortal? what gives
them sweetness after the lapse of so many ages, and vitality,
and life, so that thousands obey them, and live by them, and
die for them, false and fictitious though they be? It is
because the superstructure may be unreal, but the idea is
truth. There is a power in the very word " God " that forbids
all who invoke it to die. There is, in the very name, THAT
which preserves from putrefaction even imposture and deceit,
as the call had strength to evoke the shade of the prophet
Samuel, even though spoken by lying lips.

So is it with the remembered sanctity that still hovers
around the sites of these old religious foundations. The
dwellers in them had generally peaceful and contemplative
minds; they loved the beauties of Nature, and they chose
their abiding places with a painter's and a poet's eye.
So their memory lingers after them; the same charms that
soothed their spirits still cling to the nooks hallowed by their
retirement, heightened, and filled with holy melancholy, by
the ruins that remind us of them. The hand of violence,
that drove out from their cells the sons and daughters of
God, is powerless here. In the domain of fancy, and amid
the shadows of the past, there is a world in which exist the
people of prayer, connected with us still by a dim feeling of

our common ancestral faith, by the conscious kindred of our
human hopes and fears.   With such a spirit as this, even in
this day of professed enlightenment, there may be some who
will pause for a moment in the realities of life, to read the
following legend.

A LEGEND OF HOLY VALE.

T was Tuesday in Easter-week.

The feast had fallen late at the season of which I write, so that the beautiful valley was full of blossoms, and of green leaves, putting forth their gems timidly, as if aware of their boldness in thus venturing out so early in the world. A spell of loveliness seemed to float over the little enchanted hollow, birds sang sweetly, in the fresh and fragrant shade, leaves and buds gleamed and danced in the sunlight, and all uniting together, in one offering of material glory, and of spiritual and ineffable thankfulness, ascended to God's throne above. The orisons of Nature and of man never, peradventure, arose on high, with less of the serpent to clog their wings.

It was, indeed, a bright day, and man strove to make it brighter still. After the season of that dread Passion, succeeding the painful vigils of Lent, it was the custom of the day to indulge the people with many sports and pastimes, some of them strangely inconsistent with our ideas of ancient

mediæval discipline.   The Abbot of misrule was there, and
the dragon, and the monastic orders parodied and travestied,
and the great Tempter himself, and pretty winged children
representing, not unfitly, angels, as they may be seen, even
now, on the Continent, in the procession of the Fête Dieu.
With a keen knowledge of human nature, and somewhat too
of confidence in their own strength, the religious fraternities,
and both the secular and regular priests, allowed and even
encouraged, some apparently irreverent excesses.   These
were licensed to an unwonted extent, that day, at Holy Vale.
The mummers and *guisers* * were more numerous than usual,
and seemed to have full permission to jest, until an impious
step even intruded itself upon holy ground.   The Lady
Abbess was a dame of high birth, and of unquestioned
sanctity.   Yet the dragon of Wantley profanely ventured to
compare her to the maid Marian who figured among the
masquers, and whose condition, to tell the truth, sadly belied
her assumed character of single blessedness, the pious
superior being afflicted with an infirmity that showed itself
in an ungraceful rotundity of figure, hardly differing, to
worldly eyes, from that of the buxom matron herself.

It was not altogether the brightness of the day, nor the
celebration of Easter sports, which created this more than
usual animation and bustle.   A ceremony was being performed in the little chapel of the convent, which is always
one of solemnity and of importance in the Catholic world.
And this, too, as an event of the kind, was of no common
order.   The profession of a sister is ever an occasion of
interest for the community in which it occurs.   But the

---

* Still existing in Scilly, and called goose-dancers.

young being, now dedicated to God, was, in herself, an object of attention, from the peculiar circumstances in which she had hitherto been placed.

She was, so it was given out, an orphan, brought up in strict seclusion, under the care of an aged maiden lady, in the castle of the Earl of Cornwall, at Old Town. No one knew ought of her parentage, nor of her name. She was simply called the demoiselle Maude, and treated with such respect as, at that time, was accorded only to one of the highest rank.

To the mystery of her birth was added another and a more potent charm. She was exceeding fair, fair beyond all rivalry, rich in intellectual gifts, peerless in her lofty beauty. The wise monk, who was her preceptor, could teach her nothing more, for she had surpassed the limits of his old world lore. The brother limner, at the great Abbey of Tresco, confessed himself vanquished by her exquisite creations. The illuminated Bible, done by her, was worth a king's ransom. The broideress at St. Mary's Nunnery looked with reverence at the work of the lady Maude's hands. And with all this superiority of gifts, natural and acquired, she had the simplicity and the purity of a child. One clue only to the secret of her position was found, even by the most curious inquirers. This was in her face. Gentle and loving as she was, she had about her that which brooked no familiarity, and no intrusion. There was in her lineaments a likeness felt, but of which men never spoke. There was a sparkle of Plantagenet in her proud thoughtful eye.

Such, and in so secluded a fashion, dwelt the demoiselle Maude in the gloomy castle, a fresh and radiant spirit, budding into womanhood, and waiting, apparently, with a heart untouched, for the hour which should unite her fate to that of another. Her days were peaceful and monotonous, with little to enliven or to vary them. They were precisely the mode of existence calculated to throw a tender and confiding bosom off its guard. Full of impulse and of affection, it encountered no danger to startle it, and to teach it, by that instinctive warning sent by Providence to woman's heart, to examine its own feelings, and to analyse emotions which are never so perilous or deceitful, as when there is no suspicion of their approach. Few visiters sought the castle, and, of them, fewer still were young. Pilgrims there were, and priests, who brought tidings of the world, and talked in a simple and antique manner with the Dame de Barentin. But they took little heed of the lady Maude, as she bent over her embroidery-frame, or illumined in gold and colours, some quaint legend or heraldic device. And she was left to her own maiden meditations with none to direct or share them.

There was, indeed, in the fortress one beside herself, whom his age and position, to a certain extent, drew closer to her than to its other inmates. Jocelyn de St. Martin was the son of an old knight, who had been a former seneschal there, and was now page of honour to the Chatelaine, with a hope of admittance into the Earl's household, as an esquire. He was of the same age as the demoiselle, and they had been associates from their childhood. Oh, the danger of that seclusion, that unconscious sacrament of love, between young undoubting hearts! Not a word had been whispered on either side, not a pledge given, not a syllable of troth plighted or received, and yet, though the world dreamed not of it, the secret was no longer theirs to breathe. The youth loved that mysterious maiden, and the maiden smiled to know that she was loved.

The dream was a bright one, as bright, alas! as brief. Some passage between the two, some touch or look, some of those eloquent nothings which are the language and the soul of passion, betrayed their unspoken secret to the Dame de Barentin. She knew her duty, and acted on it instantly. The page was despatched, ostensibly, with a missive for the Earl, then residing at his castle of Launceston, but, in reality, to be the bearer of the news of this perplexing occurrence. The result of the intelligence may be conveyed in a few words. Jocelyn de St. Martin was attached to his Lord's person, as esquire, and ordered to remain and to begin his duties at once. The fate of the beautiful orphan was, to our eyes, far more sad. It did not suit the Earl's purpose that she, whom he called his ward, should be mated with one of birth inferior to her own. In those days, there was but one alternative. The demoiselle was to be the daughter of heaven. With a rich dower, as became her guardian's rank, she was at once to begin her novitiate, and to vow herself, and all her matchless charms, and her young gifted mind, at God's altar, as His virgin bride.

It was no wonder then that all was joy and festivity at Holy Vale. The Earl had intimated his desire that there should be no delay. A commission, annulling the usual period of probation, had been forwarded by John Grandison, Bishop of Exeter, to Robert Deneys, the Lord Prior of Scilly. On receiving it, notice was sent to the Dame de

Barentin, who ordered her train to horse, and conveyed her
unsuspecting charge to Holy Vale. She was there placed
in the hands of the Lady Abbess, who was henceforth
responsible for her. The fair girl was conducted to a cell,
where she was visited by the Superior, who confirmed, in
language, decided indeed, though not unkind, the suspicions
excited by the sudden journey in the maiden's breast. The
effect of such a revelation may be imagined, but cannot
be described. It was less despair than an absence of life
and its functions. It was an earthquake, crushing at once
sense and vitality. It was the mind's death, while, amid
that dreadful paralysis, the body still lived on.

But if the likeness of Plantagenet was seen upon the
brow of the unhappy girl, the spirit of that haughty race
was in her heart. She was one to die, and make no sign. If
her bosom became ice, and her being stagnated, on hearing
her doom, she never for a moment stooped to remonstrate or
to complain. She signified her willingness to proceed to the
chapel without delay. No victim ever went to the scene of
her sacrifice with a prouder step, or with a face more marble
or more serene. Not a shadow crossed it, during the whole
of that impressive solemnity. She laid aside her bridal
trappings with an air of indifference. She unloosed, and
even with her own hands gathered together, the silken
volumes of her dark hair, as the Abbess severed it, lock by
lock, from her head. When the rites were concluded, she
came forward, and received the kisses of the Abbess and of
the nuns with a cheek, calm, but so chill, that it seemed to
freeze the lips that touched it. As soon as all was done, she
retired to her cell, which was in future to be her living tomb,

as haughtily as before. Her favourite tirewoman, had, as
an act of grace, been left for a season with her, and she
came to her, and, as soon as they were alone, fell at the feet
of her lady, now only Sister Mary, with an irrepressible and
natural burst of indignation and of compassion. But the
high-born damsel raised her in silence, and kissed her brow.
There was in her eye a glassy stare, and a vacant agony, a
kind of unconscious convulsion, in her smile, that spoke of
something fearful within. But whatever she felt, she gave
it no utterance. The very evil spirit, that would have
maddened another, seemed to obey her. The poor damsel,
who loved her mistress tenderly, with the love of a common
mind, looked at her with astonishment, and could hardly
believe what she saw. The Sister took no heed of her wonder,
but gently dismissed her, and remained in her cell alone.

Whatever the secrets of that prison-house, they were
sacred, and hidden from every eye, but that of God. Nothing
was seen of Sister Mary until vespers, when she appeared in
the chapel, and petitioned, after the conclusion of the service,
that she might be allowed to remain, in prayer, before the
high altar, through the night. The request was at once
granted. It was no unusual thing, indeed; and in the case
of one thus suddenly, for some mysterious reason, cut off
from the world, it seemed natural to come unto the shrine of
the Virgin, and there to pray for support and comfort. There
could be no refuge for a bleeding heart like the love and
pity of her, whose bosom had been pierced by pangs so
great. So the Sister's prayer was accorded cheerfully, and
she was left, at the altar, to commence her painful vigil, in
communion only with the dead that slept below, and with

the Mother of God, who looked down upon her, with a smile of pity, from her niche above.

Then appeared to come upon her spirit that shadow, which the cross flings upon the bosoms of those vowed to the cloistered solitude of a religious life. The girl had departed from those walls, but the nun remained. She seldom spoke, and never complained. Her tirewoman visited her often, and was permitted to remain with her for hours in her cell, for the strict rules of the Order were tacitly remitted, in her favour. She could not be called haughty, nor was she reserved, but there was no fellowship between the other Sisters and herself, and, it may be unconsciously, she occupied a place, both in feeling and intellect, which they could not reach. She never mingled with them. Instead of the usual equality of the conventual life, when by chance they met her moving about, looking so proud, yet so woebegone withal, they made her a hurried reverence, and passed on. Her only occupation seemed to be the care of a rose-bush, said to have some miraculous properties, and consecrated to the Virgin. It was from this bush that the place was called Holy Vale. One of its flowers was deemed to have the power, if worn, to preserve its bearer from mortal sin. And one of its crimson buds was always borne upon her bosom, for the bush had the gift of perpetual spring, and blossomed through the entire year.

So passed away the months of her novitiate. Winter—such as winter is in this land of the aloe, the myrtle, and the geranium—was melting before the smile of spring. The day was approaching when the irrevocable black veil was to be assumed. The demeanour of the novice was unchanged.

It was as cold, as formal, and as still as ever. Her faithful tirewoman spent with her the eve of the fatal day, and when Sister Mary had dismissed her from the cloister gate, after vespers, she asked permission to spend in the chapel the solemn night, that was to usher in for her as solemn a dawn. The Abbess gave the desired leave, with her blessing on the head of the fair nun, so soon to be affianced to heaven, by the last awful tie. She went alone, through the holy place, to the high altar, and there was seen, by those who casually observed her, like a prostrate statue, absorbed in an agony of prayer. There they parted from her, but, on the morrow, they sought her there in vain. She left no relic of her presence. They found no traces of her flight. One thing only showed that she had been lately near. By the rosebush of the Virgin was found a bough broken off, and thrown down upon the ground, one opening bud alone being taken from its stem. Save this slight indication of her taste, and of the tenderness of a crushed heart for even an inanimate thing, her fate and her history were a void. The wrath of the stern Earl was terrible, but it was as vain as the quiet lamentations of the sisterhood. She, whom they deemed a perjured nun, was gone, and, apparently, gone for ever. The solemn beauty of her pale countenance was missed for a time, but, as no tidings of the fugitive were received, the impression caused by her loss waxed fainter and yet more faint. The name of the fugitive was scarcely ever mentioned; her empty place was filled up by another; her memory was, as it were, a tale that is told.

Years glided along, and passed lightly, as time ever passes, over the community of Holy Vale. Yet still, even in a religious society, the hand of the great leveller comes down, gathering, one by one, the human blossoms on the tree of life. The sisters were called from their simple duties, and left the grey walls for a home more lasting, but scarcely more silent or more sad. The stately Abbess laid down her life and her authority together, and bequeathed her mild sceptre to her successor. Those who had known Sister Mary, and had pondered tearfully over her disappearance, at the moment when they deemed her about to win an immortal crown, were removed from the scene. Two or three only, at an advanced age, still lingered on. They spoke sometimes of the mystery of Sister Mary's flight, but all hope of clearing it up was gone. The register of the angel on high could alone solve the terrible problem. To earth, and to mortal eyes, it was, apparently, a sealed volume, to be opened only by a mightier hand than that of man.

So, however, it was not fated to be. The eve of Easter Tuesday had again come round, and had fallen late in the year, on exactly the same day as that on which Sister Mary had been lost to God and to them, as it seemed, for ever. The eve of the same Tuesday had once more brought its duties, and its religious observances; for a solemn mass was performed for her who had so unaccountably vanished, and Heaven was entreated for her. It was observed that the rose-bush put forth its earliest and choicest blossoms, in loving profusion. A spirit of peace, and a sacred blessing, appeared to be floating over the hallowed spot. During vespers, a sweet voice seemed to mingle with the choir, as though an angel sang.

Next morning the great doors of the chapel were thrown

open, as was usual on occasions of state, for matins. The Abbess entered, at the head of her train, but the building was not untenanted. It was already occupied by One, upon whom was impressed the grandeur, and the sanctity, conferred by an immortal power from its contact with that which is mortal. Death, that consecrates by its touch, and hallows even while it slays, had been busy there.

A form lay upon the highest step, before the great altar, its hands clasped upon its bosom in the attitude of prayer, and so marble-like and motionless that it might have been deemed an effigy on a tomb. There was no mistaking its dread repose, nor its rigid limbs, nor the stony expression of its upturned face. Death was frozen in its lineaments of rare beauty, but the expression was as calm and child-like as though they were but composed in sleep, and a sweet smile played about the lips, fixed there, perhaps, by the guardian angel, that bore away the departing spirit from a frame so fair. The form was one of early womanhood, and was clothed in the dress of a novice of the house. Upon the cold bosom, and on the heart that throbbed no more with life, was placed a rose bud, apparently long gathered, but yet as fresh as though newly plucked from its stem. The sisters crowded round the figure, sleeping in its awful loveliness. The two aged nuns recognised it at once. It was their lost sister, Mary.

They buried her where she lay. It was vain to ask by what miracle she had been preserved and given back, in her pure and perfect innocence, for by her outward beauty they might be assured of that within. Perhaps the rose bud had guarded her from temptation, and had imparted to her

strength to resist it. So they committed her to the dust,
with her body sinless and undefiled, and raised above her a
marble monument; and the fame of Holy Vale, and of its
sacred flower, flourished in the land.

Save those survivors of her sisterhood, there remained,
indeed, none to inquire into her fate. Men spoke of a
secret passage, leading from the chapel to St. Mary's, at
Old Town, by which she had escaped, and joined her
faithful tirewoman; but these surmises led to no result. The
stern Earl was dead. Jocelyn de St. Martin had died too, in
harness, warring against the infidels. When she thus came
back, raised, as it were, from the grave, only to be restored
to it for ever, she had as little affinity to the old and feeble
nuns, as she had felt, when, more than a generation before,
she had walked in haughty solitude, beneath that roof. Her
presence there troubled them, with its unearthly brightness,
and its strange gift of youth, and the contrast of its angelic
freshness with their wrinkled and forbidding brows.

So they buried her where she lay, in the odour of her
sanctity, and in her undying beauty. At the Reformation,
the black marble slab, placed above her rest, was destroyed,
but, according to tradition, it bore these words alone,—

> " Cy git Marie
> Priez pour elle."

Amid the general dearth of local tradition, and of relics of all sorts,
Holy Vale has rather a distinguished place. It can show not only an
ancient well, from whose properties it perhaps derives its name, and a
range of orchards and gardens, which may have belonged to a religious
establishment, for they have a decidedly conventual appearance, but also
a portion of some fabric, which is of incontestable antiquity. This is

the top of a freestone arch, once forming part of a doorway or of a window, but now covering the entrance of a pig-sty. It may be seen behind the first house, on the left-hand side of the road, as it approaches the little hamlet from Hugh Town. There are, likewise, many other wells, in places where now no houses exist, but where there must formerly, from the very presence of such things, have been both dwellings and inhabitants. A resident at Holy Vale has in his possession a curious and interesting relic of the past. It is an old chair, bought at a sale of the furniture of Star Castle, and said to have been equally honoured with that celebrated by Sir Walter Scott in " Old Mortality," and so much prized by Lady Margaret Bellenden, in the tower of Tillietudlem, for " His Most Gracious Majesty, Charles the Second," once sate in it.

CHAPTER VIII.

BRYHER.

HIS morning I went on an excursion to Bryher. It is one of the inhabited islands, lying between Tresco (to which it is joined by the sands at low water) and Samson. Probably all three were formerly one; for, as I have observed elsewhere, the space now covered by the sea is full of walls and enclosures. The fate of St. Mary's has clearly been anticipated here.

The distance between the Quay at Hugh Town, and Oliver Cromwell's Castle, which is built in the channel parting Bryher from Tresco, and on the shores of the latter, is just three miles. So wide is the fine pool of St. Mary's. I made the passage in about twenty minutes, under sail, with a stiff breeze. I had a six-oared gig, that literally flew over the waves. The craft of this kind here are proverbially good, and ours formed no exception to the rule. On our return, with a jumping sea, and the wind dead ahead, our six stout islanders did the whole space, from point to point, in three-quarters of an hour, without shipping a drop of water. The men were proud of their boat, but they said that there was another in the island worth two of her.

Bryher contains at the present time thirty families, and one hundred and nineteen inhabitants. Its average length is about a mile and a half; its breadth scarcely half a mile. The ground rises abruptly in every part from the shore, into which the sea is visibly eating its way. The whole of Bryher consists only of three hundred and thirty acres, a great deal of which is still uncultivated. To the east of the declivity called Gweal Hill, from the opposite islet of that name,* is a pool of fresh water, covering two or three acres. On the north-west side is a pretty spring, said to be useful for medicinal purposes. It is so situated under the cliff, that the sun never shines upon it. The steep hill opposite Samson is named from it " Samson hill " and has, or rather had, on its summit, three barrows, parts of which have been removed. These, as far as I could learn, are all the objects of interest to be seen, and they do not present a very varied list. But the resources of Nature are less limited, and on a far grander scale. Her " treasure caves and cells " need no fostering hand to draw forth or to develope them. Of the six inhabited islands, none is more full of stern and wild beauty than Bryher. And though every carn, and rock, and headland, has its name, to enumerate them would be

---

* This is a peculiarity in the local nomenclature. Samson hill of Bryher is the one in Bryher opposite Samson. Bryher hill in Samson, or of Samson, is so called for a similar reason.

only to present to the eye a list of unmeaning appellations,
uncouth as the scenes to which they are applied, and to our
ears as dead as the language of the names they bear, which,
with its children, has passed away for ever.

The gap between historical and mythical times, between
the bright sunlight, and the shadowy poetry of the mountain
mist, is shown clearly in the names of places here. These
islands, whether formerly of greater or of less extent, were
once thickly peopled. The graves rise up in witness of this
fact. Every point, and carn, has its distinct appellation.
There is not a solitary hill, nor a grey tomb, which has not
received the baptism of one of those ancient words, which
have in them so much beauty and expression. But not one
of those words belongs to an era within the memory of man.
The fount from which they were named is as unknown as
the lips that christened them. The antique dweller on
Minalto, and Mincarlo, felt the influence of this genial
climate, and the spirit in his heart found utterance in his
tongue, and so, in the rich varieties of his forgotten vocabu-
lary, he discovered those terms which we now admire. But
they are all distant, and unreal as a dream. To reach them,
we must leap over a gulf, not of years, but of centuries.
The Phœnician, the Greek, the Roman, the men of the
dark ages, have left no trace of their language. We do not
recognize their presence by one phrase that sounds to our
ears like a familiar friend. The Briton only, with his
Druid, comes before us, and shows us the relics of his
religion, and bids us confess the accents of his tongue, and
claims these domains for his own. The fact is singular, but,
stripped of all colouring, it is true. When we leave the

words of a language that is mythological, we come to those
of to-day. There is no interval. There is no resting-place
for thought, nor for speculation, between us and Arviragus.
When we quit the Briton, we come to Banfield, and Toll,
and Leg; we leave Kunobelin, and find ourselves with
to-day. There is in the hands of the Proprietor a Terrier of
the Islands, of the time of the Commonwealth, and there
are in it, I think, only three names extant here at the present
time. Probably a change so rapid and so sweeping is
without a parallel.

On landing, I walked up the beach, and entered two
houses belonging to the fishermen. Their extreme comfort
struck me forcibly. The kitchen of the one in which I
remained a short time was furnished with every requisite,
and the sitting-room was filled with glass, and china, and
even with some humble attempts at ornament. There were,
in a corner cupboard, several antique silver spoons. The
dress of the host and his wife was good and clean. I may
say, *en passant*, that Woodley's account of the extreme
poverty of the Scillonians—if in his time it were correct—
is now so no longer. On every side are palpable evidences
of prosperity and well doing. From all I hear, however,
this state of things is of no long standing. The change has
been wrought in the last few years, but it seems likely to be
permanent, as it is complete.

When I quitted the cottage, I was joined by a respectable
man, who stated that he was a farmer, and offered to accom-
pany me on my walk. We went first in the direction of the
little church, built, at an expense of £250, by the Society
for promoting the erection and enlargement of churches.

There is a meeting-house on the hill above, but it is now shut up. Service is performed here by the Curate from Tresco, who crosses from thence in a boat, every Sunday afternoon. A little further on is the Coast-guard Station. Following the road, we ascended the hill, which is bold and steep. Most of the ground is covered with furze, and affords pasture to a few mountain ponies and sheep, as well as to some cross-bred Alderney cows. In the sheltered nooks are always planted early potatoes, which are bought up at a price varying from six-pence a pound to £1 : 5 : 0 a bushel,* and are sent to Covent Garden market. They form the chief reliance of the people, and great distress was caused by their failure, in the disastrous years of the potato disease. The land is of excellent quality, and lets at from one to two pounds per acre. I saw a good deal trenched with sea-weed for manure, and prepared thus for sowing barley, which is generally done in the first week in April.

We ascended the hill, while I made these observations, until we gained a considerable altitude, and then paused to look around. The scene was indeed strikingly magnificent. Facing us was Hugh Town, low as Venice in its lagoons. Below was the pool of St. Mary's, in whose anchorage a whole navy might ride in safety. To the left was St. Martin, and nearer us, on the same side, Tresco, its Abbey gleaming in the sun, its pool sleeping like a sheet of molten silver, and its grounds forming a picturesque contrast to the sterile solitude around. On our extreme right was St. Agnes, surrounded by its archipelago of rocks, and, nearer still, Samson, the population of which is fast being removed, as

---

* The price this year was £1 : 15 : 0 per bushel.

opportunities offer, to St. Mary's, only three or four families now remaining on the island. Add, to this combination of all that is simply grand in art and in Nature, a blue sky, a breeze just sufficient to ripple the surface of the bay, and to produce what Œschylus calls " its countless smiles," a sea almost as azure as that of the Mediterranean, with sands dazzlingly white, and whiter still by contrast with the objects around, and there is a picture before you which it would be difficult to equal, and impossible to surpass. My companion told me that, near where we were then standing, he once broke with the plough into a barrow. He found there ten or a dozen pots, or jars, full of a kind of gritty dust, exhaling a very fetid odour. The whole earth around was unctuous and black, and smelt unpleasantly. As soon as the atmosphere was admitted, the vessels mouldered away, and no relic of them was left. The islands abound in remains of the kind, giving indisputable evidence of the existence, heretofore, of a far more numerous population than of late years, as do the circles, and cromlechs, and kist-vaens, and menhirs; for where there were so many temples, there must have been both priests and worshippers. I have been much surprised, however, at the almost total absence of traditionary tales, both here and in Cornwall; and at the little interest seemingly taken by the natives in their antiquities. Ask one of them the history of a ruin, and in most cases his reply will be, like that of Lord Melbourne when prime minister, " I am sure I don't know," though he seldom adds " but I'll ask."

 · As we turned to descend the hill, a bend in the road brought us opposite to Tresco, separated from Bryher by

Grimsby, or Grimsey, channel. Cromwell's Castle lay before us. My guide told me that the ruins on the hill above were the remains of a still more ancient fortress, which was battered down by Cromwell, who then built the tower below, to command the passage. The Protector, however, was never here. In 1651 Sir John Grenville, after a gallant defence, surrendered the Islands to the parliamentary troops, under Sir George Ayscough and Admiral Blake; Prince Charles having previously resided here for some time.

It is singular how the reputation of the Great Puritan warrior is always connected with gloom and destruction, though his civil government was wise and firm. It was not so with Napoleon. He created everywhere, and laid the foundation of the present greatness of France. But Cromwell is always remembered as a destroyer. To his hand was attributed all the ruin worked during the civil wars, even in places which he never visited. You go to a cathedral, and are told that he battered it down, though he was then warring far away. You see a wide breach in a decayed curtain, and his tremendous name is connected with the storming of the place. You are shown a relic of him. It is a basket-hilted sword, or a buff coat, or a half pike. His associations are all of strife. He is the embodied actor of the Rebellion. His memory is indeed " the sword of the Lord, and of Gideon." In the tale of those bloody fights, when the wounded of the Cavaliers were butchered by those who boasted, " that they did not the Lord's work negligently," his name only is mentioned, in history and legend, as the one that smote and spared not. The Saracen mother that frightened her spoiled child, and the Saracen rider that threatened his horse, with the awful name of Richard, acted exactly as my guide of to-day acted, when he pointed to the fortalice below us, as it lay gloomily on the dim shore, and told me that Cromwell built it, from the ruins he had himself made.

The scene was suitable to the tale. The shadows of evening were coming down fast. St. Mary's pool was vanishing from the eye. The wind swept sullenly up Grimsby channel, and howled around the decayed walls of the fort. The only sound heard was the scream of the sea-birds, as they winged their way back to the cliffs of the off isles. The spirit of the Old Protector might have brooded over the castle that bore his name. As I gazed, it faded slowly from my sight, and was no longer seen. I wished my guide good night, and returned in silence to my boat.

CHAPTER IX.

TRESCO.

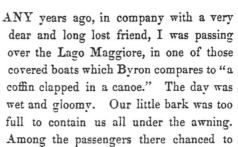ANY years ago, in company with a very dear and long lost friend, I was passing over the Lago Maggiore, in one of those covered boats which Byron compares to "a coffin clapped in a canoe." The day was wet and gloomy. Our little bark was too full to contain us all under the awning. Among the passengers there chanced to be a French gentleman (or rather a Frenchman), and his bride, a pretty and delicate woman. When the rain began in earnest, the gallant Gaul squeezed himself into a place under cover, taking with him all his wraps, and leaving his wife to the sole protection of a small parasol. We gave up to her one of our seats, and it was quite touching to see the warmth with which the worthy husband thanked us.

After a little while the mist rolled away from the bosom of the lake. Shadows and gleams of pale light floated over its surface. Then the blue haze of the sky grew more distinct, and the sun of Italy came forth, and Isola Bella lay before our eyes, glittering with dew, and bathed in the glories of a summer day.

There are scenes in our lifetime that strike us forcibly, and then seem to die and, as it were, be buried, embalmed in the freshness of their memory. They are apparently forgotten, as though they had never been. But long afterwards, perhaps at a great distance, with seemingly nothing to form a link between the present and the almost ideal past, some accident calls forth the associations that are sleeping only, not dead, and our impressions of other days arise again before us, with all the fidelity of visible life. It is perhaps a glimmering, or a reflection of the gift of immortality, which we inherit with the likeness, and after the image, of Him who made us. It may be a fine sparkle of His omniscience, a fragment of the ruin of our angelic nature, a shadow from the closed gate of paradise. But so it is. Sometimes, unexpectedly, a scene of our old existence glides back, and forms a part of our busy Now. This happened to me to-day. When walking in the gardens of Tresco Abbey, I was again, in imagination, at Isola Bella. The flood of years, that formed, up to that moment, an impassable barrier between me and it, was swept away. The life of other days came back, with a gush of young feelings, and a warm remembrance of one who is now no more. I realized Longfellow's beautiful idea, on passing over the Rhine alone, in the same boat which had formerly borne three happy comrades :—

> " Take oh ! boatman, thrice thy fee,
> Take, I give it willingly,
> For, invisible to thee,
> Spirits twain have crossed with me."

In saying so little of Tresco Abbey, and of its lovely gardens,* I put great violence on my feelings. But I am bound both in courtesy, in gratitude, and as a matter of justice, to consult the wishes of others. And, in deference to them, I pass over in silence much that I should otherwise have been delighted to notice and to praise. It is due to myself to say so much, and it is equally due to others to say no more. †

The relative size and importance of these Islands have changed materially, even since the days of Leland, who speaks of Tresco as the largest of the group. ‡ It was then doubtless united to Bryher and Samson on the one hand, and perhaps to St. Martin's on the other. Now it is not more than six miles in circumference. Its population has equally diminished. It must have been very numerously peopled in former times, from the visible evidence of

---

* The geranium hedges are so magnificent, being in some places from fourteen to sixteen feet high, as almost to verify and realize the pardonable boast of one who had the honour of the Islands at heart, and was reproached with their want of wood, " Indeed, we heat our ovens with our geranium faggots ! "

† My friend, Mr. J. G. Moyle, the resident medical man here, must pardon me if he is the unlucky exception to my general rule of avoiding all mention of names. His great talent, as an artist, is so well known to his friends, that any praise of mine would be superfluous. But, as an act of gratitude, I cannot help saying that he has presented me with a work of his, which I value as much for the kindness that prompted the gift, and for its intrinsic worth, as for the associations it recalls. It is an oil-painting of Tresco Abbey, taken at sunset. The building, and the landscape around, are bathed in the purple haze of twilight, while its soft glow is caught and fixed upon the canvass, with a spirit, and a dreamy poetical beauty, the effect of which it is hardly possible to describe.

‡ See appendix.

sepulchral remains, though Pliny says that there was a prejudice in favour of an insular burying-place. But it is difficult to account for the falling off in the number of the inhabitants, and of the inhabited houses. Troutbeck says that there were, within the memory of man, only twelve families in Tresco. There were in his time seventy-four dwellings. Now the population is about four hundred and fifty souls. Samson, Bryher, and Tresco, number together six hundred.

The evidence of ancient populousness is too strong to admit of doubt or contradiction, but the causes of decline are beyond man's power to trace. History is utterly silent, and tradition nearly so. But we cannot hesitate to believe that, at no very distant period, many, if not all, of these isolated rocks, have formed one great main land, teeming with wealth and richness.* Whether an earthquake has wrought this melancholy change, or whether the sea, gradually rising, has submerged the lower grounds, it is impossible to say. When the tide is out, says Troutbeck, a man may walk from St. Mary's to St. Martin's, and from thence to Tresco. Ruins of houses, as well as the remains of hedges, are frequently discovered beneath the sand, many feet below water mark. In the middle of Crow sound, a fine regular pavement of large flat stones is seen, about eight feet under low water, at spring tides. But it is useless to dwell further on this point. At present Tresco, as the seat of Government, is rising fast in power and prosperity. The first thing I saw in it was a steam mill. The next was a

---

* See Borlase.

servant in livery, kindly sent to meet and conduct me to the
Abbey.   Dogs of a rare breed were basking in the sun upon
the broad road, before the gates.   Pheasants rose upon the
wing, and flew along the margin of the great pool, which,
covering fifty acres and upwards, reflected in its bosom the
hill, rich with gorse in full bloom, and with exotic shrubs.
As I walked onwards, fancy drew me away from the present
to the times of Eld, when a great continent occupied the site
of these romantic rocks and vales.   A turn in the carriage-
way brought me in sight of the house.   There, before the
Reformation, stood perchance a far loftier fabric.   Though
attached to the Monastery of Tavistock, the Abbey of Tresco
was yet not inferior to some of the proudest religious establishments in England.   As I looked upon its successor, I recalled
many circumstances connected with its records.   The reader
will, I hope, pardon me, if I turn aside from passing events,
and from the realities of to-day, to lay before him a legend
of Iniscaw, or Tresco, called—

THE KNIGHT AND THE DWARF.

THE KNIGHT AND THE DWARF.

 T was a goodly pile, that Abbey of St. Nicholas in Tresco, or, as it was then called, Iniscaw,* embosomed, like a picture, in the setting of its brown hill, gleaming with heather blooms, and with golden furze. In every direction around it lay hamlets, and comfortable farm-houses, surrounded by cultivated lands, and meadows of deep green. Surely the good Fathers owned a fair heritage; and the state of their dependencies showed that, while enjoying a pleasant lot themselves, they dealt gently and kindly with those beneath their sway.

So was it in those days. Not then, as now, was the pilgrim or the wayfarer compelled to seek a venal welcome at the wayside inn. Not then, as now, was hospitality only to be bought. The first of the monastic virtues, and the one most worthily practised, was charity. Far and wide, through Christendom, were scattered those memorials of our Fathers' piety, those solemn Abbeys and Priories, buried in the dim religious shade of trees coeval with the foundation of the

---

* Ynys-scao, Isle of Elders.

buildings, over which they bent so gracefully. And wherever arose one of those grey piles, there was to be found a sacred hospitality,—a kindness dispensed alike to rich and poor,—a practical lesson of love for God and man. Under the shelter of those walls grew up a loving tenantry, and, still lower in the scale, a body of peasants, connected with their superiors by ties of affection, and of reverence, and of benefits, both given and received. Go now to Scilly, and seek out the Abbey gates. Where are they? In a bright garden, full of the luxuriant beauty of tropical flowers and shrubs, you pass by two glorious aloes, and behold a grey wall, and a fine pointed arch. Is there anything more? Yes, there is yet one relic more. A few antique graves are scattered around; for this place, redolent of perfumes, was the burial ground of the Abbey. There is nothing here to remind you of death. The ground is covered with a Mosaic of bright-eyed blossoms, and the air is heavy with fragrance. These grey stones, and ancient tombs, are all that is left of the great Abbey. If you would ask for the old Catholic hospitality on this spot, as of yore, it must be from the dead, whose mansions are lying about, and whose spirits may, peradventure, brood over the scene of a majesty decayed, and spoiled, and utterly laid waste. A hind, passing by, looks at you through the mossy arch ; the wind moans round the fragments that remain, and the saddened stranger, gazing for a moment on the ruins of God's house, remembers what it once has been, and, with a sigh, turns sorrowfully away.

Not such, however, was the appearance of the stately Abbey of St. Nicholas, in Tresco, about the middle of the

fourteenth century, on one fine morning, in May. The peace
and dignified tranquillity, that generally characterised it,
were gone. All was hot haste, and confusion, and hurrying
to and fro. The reverend brethren paced the lofty walls, or
passed from chamber to court, and from court to chamber,
or gazed through the great gates, now opened wide, with
distress and terror painted upon their countenances. From
time to time a string of cattle, or of sheep, or of beasts of
burden, entered the sacred precincts, while their drivers,
accompanied by troops of women and children, outvied each
other in their dismal tales, to which the monks listened, with
faces as pale as those of the speakers. Every now and then,
amid the disarray and uproar, there arrived a band of armed
men, headed by some one of higher rank, who held lands of
the Abbey by bridle and spear, and came, with his vassals,
to discharge his feudal devoirs, by protecting it, and doing
battle in its cause.

As troop after troop filed in, the military garnishing of
the place became very respectable; and a casual observer
would have smiled at the idea of danger to a stronghold so
well defended. But the peril that menaced it was apparently
of no common kind. In spite of the formidable muster of
men-at-arms, and spearmen, and archers, and cross-bow men,
that crowded the Abbey courts, the terror that existed before
their coming did not seem to cease, nor were its inmates
reassured by their presence. In the midst of the discordant
shouting, and the absence of all order, and of all authority,
the monks, and peasants, and troops, were mixed up together
in a medley of inextricable confusion. No one was there of
rank or of talent sufficient to entitle him to take the lead, as

well as for others to acquiesce in his superiority. The only
person to whom men would naturally have turned was the
Abbot. But the good priest was well-nigh beside himself
with dismay. He moved backwards and forwards, amid
the crowd, as it ebbed and flowed, like a man paralyzed by
some great shock. " Monseigneur St. Nicholas," was his
constant and dolorous cry, "pity us, and come to our aid.
Save us, for we perish, and there is none to deliver us.
Monseigneur St. Nicholas, pray for us!"

The prayers and ejaculations of the worthy Abbot were,
naithless, of small avail, towards the restoration of the peace
so rudely disturbed. As drove, and flock, and horseman,
and footman, passed into the monastery, it became evident
that, spacious as were its limits, they would soon prove
insufficient to accommodate the new comers. The retainers
of the house, armed and equipped for service, stood in
groups, or seated themselves to rest, here and there, while
their leaders seemed to have abandoned the idea,—if such a
one ever existed,—of establishing some discipline. After
a few ineffectual efforts, they let things take their course, and
looked listlessly on. Now an order was issued to send forth
scouts, to ascertain what was passing on the side from which
danger was dreaded, and then it was countermanded, until
thin lines of bluish smoke dotted the landscape, in ominous
proximity to the Abbey, and the command was repeated, but
it was unheard, or, if heard, unheeded. From time to time
the man, stationed on the top of the great tower, as a look-
out, reported the progress of the enemy, and, at every fresh
intimation of the spoiler's approach, the Abbot's agony increased, and his appeals to Monseigneur St. Nicholas became

more incessant. One or two of the chief tenants tried to
arrest the disorder that prevailed, and to induce the Abbot
to second them. There could be but one result, were this
state of things to continue. They saw this, and made an
effort to amend matters. " Holy Father," they said, " it is
time to hang out from the tower the great banner of the
house, and to man the walls." But to these appeals the
priest turned a deaf ear. His reply was still the same.
" God, and Monseigneur St. Nicholas, be our aid!" he cried,
" what can I, or what can any man, do in such a strait?
Lo, I am a man of peace, what then know I of the battle or
of blood? I will not trust in the arm of flesh, but in the
weapons of the Spirit, and of prayer. Monseigneur St.
Nicholas, aid us!" And the good followers of the Abbey,
thorougly disheartened, shrugged their shoulders, and, great
as might be the Abbot's faith in the help of his Patron Saint,
seemed themselves to share but little in his devout trust.
They went back to their men, with a look on their weather-
beaten brows that spake, as plainly as glance ever spake, of
minds made up to meet the impending danger, but of hope-
lessness, and utter despair of success.

One of these men, who was past the prime of life, and
had apparently seen some service, from the broad scar that
traversed his sun-burnt forehead, was disposed to give vent to
his discontent in words. He gazed sternly round upon the
increasing crowds, whose din had become almost deafening,
with no friendly or placable look. Then his eye wandered to
the figure of the Abbot, who was standing still, in a lamentable
state of bewilderment and indecision. " Aye," muttered the
stout veteran, half in soliloquy, and half addressing himself

to his companion, " Heaven helps him who helps himself.
My old captain, Sir John Chandos, whose one eye nothing
ever escaped (on his soul be peace!), could do nought with
such a scum as this.   Would that I and my men were safely
back, and housed within the walls of my manoir at Samson.
There might I at least strike a good stroke for mine own, or
make some composition with these rovers.   But the Abbot
can neither fight, nor bid others do it for him.   Marry, he
will find his prayers but a sorry defence against lance-heads,
and sword points, and blazing brands.   I would give the
value of ten arpents of my best land, sith the fight must be
fought against such odds, if Bras-de-fer were but here."

Most of this long monologue had fallen unheeded upon
the tympanum of the Abbot's ears, but they caught its conclusion.   The effect was electric.   The name pronounced
seemed even as is a beacon to a storm-tost mariner,—as a
straw to a drowning man.   He was in a moment absorbed
by the one idea that he had just received, as though it were
an inspiration from on high.   Turning to William le Poer,
the speaker, he demanded, in an agitated voice, where Bras-
de-fer was, and bade them summon him instantly.   The
attempt indeed was made, but it was made in vain.   To the
cries that resounded on every side, coupled with his name,
no answer was returned, save the significant one of silence.
Bras-de-fer was nowhere to be found ; and the Abbot's
distress grew again to a height that would have been amusing,
had it not also been sincere and real.

A new cause for alarm was now superadded to those already
existing.   The warder on the tower announced the appearance
of one of the scouts, who had been sent out to explore the

neighbourhood. At the same moment with the announce-
ment, in he rode, spurring his panting hob, or cob, whose
bloody sides, and foaming mouth, gave tokens of his rider's
headlong speed. In he rode, breathless, and almost without
tongue to tell his tale. The crowd, as he entered, made
way for him silently, and then closed round him, and asked
him for his tidings. They were soon told. The fleet of
pirates, whose threatened presence had frightened the Islands
from their propriety, was the naval portion of those dreaded
and detested routiers, who scorched their track upon the
shores they visited with sword and flame. Like locusts,
they had passed over the fair lands of France and Italy, and
left a desert behind them. The fatal legacy of the English
wars, they had lingered on, sometimes, by the temptation of
pay and plunder, bribed into the service of one of the
neighbouring sovereigns ; sometimes put down by the united
forces of the crown, and of the great Barons ; and, sometimes,
for lack of prey to feed upon, dwindling into mere herds
of robbers. Still, however, they continued to exist, and
were ever ready, at times of civil discord, to start up
into unnatural strength and stature. Such a portentous
gathering was it that swept, like a hurricane, over the
ancient Hesperides, the Fortunate Isles, now called Scilly,
and threatened pillage and death against the fair Abbey of
Tresco. This formed the substance of the hobbler's tale.
The modern Vikingir, the routiers, had swooped upon the
rich booty, from far and near. Their united bands, seizing
upon all the shipping within their reach, came down upon
the monastery, in which, in addition to wealth of its own,
was deposited much belonging to others. Those, however,

who put trust in its broad moat and frowning towers,
might now feel some apprehension for the result. Fenced
cities had stooped, and given way, before these terrible bands.
Princes had condescended to treat with them, and to pay a
species of black-mail for their protection or their forbearance.
And now, like a multitude of ravening wolves, they made
right for the treasures of the Sanctuary, even as the Assyrian
yearned for the wealth of Zion. They disdained to summon
a place, the wealth of which gave a spur to their covetousness, and which for its weakness they despised. They made,
therefore, no overtures to the monks. Their terms were
simply surrender and submission. Between that, and resistance to the uttermost, there was no medium. The choice
was given to the community, and a dreadful choice it was.
Like the memorable message and reply at Saragossa, the
leader of the robbers might have demanded an instant
capitulation; and who was there, amid that panic-stricken
mob, to reply to his insolent summons, in the words of
Palafox to the Frenchman, " Guerra al cuchillo "—War to
the knife ?

When it was known that the great host of routiers had
disembarked, and were coming in force against the Abbey,
their advanced parties being seen already on the side of
Bryher hill, the very magnitude of the danger produced a
sort of calm. Men were stunned into order, and began to
feel the necessity of subordination. By a sort of tacit and
spontaneous movement, some of those better equipped and
disciplined fell in together, and proceeded to man the wall.
Some mangonels, and military machines, were carried thither,
and prepared for use. The old captain, William le Poer,

took advantage of this mute submission to post the troops
to the best advantage, and to place the non-combatants
in a situation where they would, at least, be out of the way.
After doing all in his power, he had descended to consult
the Abbot on some doubtful point, and had just found the
reverend Father in the great court, when both soldier and
priest were startled by a shout, that made the welkin ring,
and was re-echoed by the grey pile around them. The stout
veteran cut short his speech, and listened for a repetition of
the cries. When it came, he then knew the reason for that
burst of enthusiasm. None can feel the value of an able
leader, when the question is one of life and death, so well as
a soldier. And therefore it was with no common joy or
exultation that he gathered the meaning of that warlike
welcome. It was the greeting of his followers to a well
proved chief. William le Poer's heart leapt within him, as
the air shook with one unanimous acclaim,—" Bras-de-fer,
Bras-de-fer, St. Nicholas for Bras-de-fer!"

"Marry," said the worthy Abbot, " Sir Bras-de-fer is
somewhat slow in making his appearance, but right glad am
I that he is come at last. Peradventure he has gathered his
vassals, and the knaves loitered, and delayed the good
knight. I trust that his band is neither scanty nor ill-
equipped, for he holdeth broad lands of the Church, and,
as a certain Father hath it — " here he broke off, and stood
with silent amazement, gazing on the scene that presented
itself.

First, his hands bound behind his back with a cord, his
head drooped in a hang-dog fashion upon his breast, and
his whole figure bearing unmistakeable signs of dogged,

insolent, ruffianly fear, came a man, clad in half-armour,
but possessing no offensive weapons.   His steel cap, or
salade, as well as his breast and back plate, were stained
with rust and dirt, and his swarthy face, and untrimmed
beard, and garments of buff, were in perfect keeping with
the rest of his equipments.   He looked what he really was,
a common routier, or condottiero, of the day.   Behind him,
and quickening his pace occasionally by a sharp prick of
his lance, rode one of a far different stamp.   As if in contrast to the mere mercenary, the base trafficker in war,
appeared one of those martial and chivalrous warriors,
whom Froissart painted and loved so spiritedly, followed, as
his whole train, by two well appointed esquires.   Of great
stature, far exceeding the usual height of men, and of
enormous strength, he yet sate his powerful Norman destrier,
with the ease and grace of a page mounting his first war-
horse.   He was clad in complete armour, and over his
bright bassinet, and shadowing his open and honest features,
floated a long white plume.   His whole bearing was a model
of noble and manly vigour, and the very smile upon his
firm resolute mouth, was an augury of victory.   The fathers
of the men of those days, who had fought in the wars of
the giants, when England and France had met so often in
stricken fields, face to face, looked frequently upon such
champions, and spoke of Edward Plantagenet in his black
mail, and Chandos, and Audley, and Felton; and, on the
opposite side, the brothers du Guesclin, and the Marshals
de Lignac and de Passac, and Comminges, and Perigord,
who, though simple Counts only, dared to send their gloves
in defiance to the Prince of Wales.   In the days of which

I am writing, however, the heroic mould was well nigh worn
out. In the words of Ariosto,—

"Natura la fece, et poi ruppe la stampa."

The eleventh Louis loved chivalry but little, and if he was
served by such men as Dunois, it was almost against his
will. Even in the wars then terminated, few had seen a
more perfect or a more gallant cavalier than he, who, with
his visor up, and with his brave spirit stamped upon his
face, rode into the Abbey court, amid waving of caps, and
gratulatory shouts, and a wild welcome, uttered in chorus
by a hundred tongues.

Bras-de-fer spake not a word in reply, but threw a bright
glance over the crowd, and then went straight up to the
Abbot. The holy man was paralyzed. He gazed in utter
astonishment upon the good knight, then upon his prisoner,
and lastly upon his esquires. When, however, he was
convinced of the reality of what he saw; when, by the
existence of his senses, he became certain that the four, now
grouped in his presence, composed the whole attendance of his
redoubted vassal, astonishment gave place to anger,—anger
too great to find expression in words. All that he could
say was, "Monseigneur St. Nicholas, aid us!" in a manner
so ludicrously plaintive, as to bring a smile on the lips of
Bras-de-fer.

"Aye" said he "my Lord Abbot, I trust he will help us,
for we lack his aid, and, if legends tell truth, he was a rude
adversary in his day. Do ye know with whom ye have to
deal?" As no one answered the question, he continued.
"If all the fiends of hell were let loose, saving your presence,
my reverend friend, they could have no more fitting leader

than the master-spirit of that murthering and pillaging
horde. As I rode in, I chanced to light on this villainous
routier, overthrew him horse and man, and got from him all
the news he could furnish. I am ill at telling a story, so the
sum of the whole is this. All the sea-kings, as they are
pleased to call themselves, are collected in one band, to fall
upon us, and at their head is that devil incarnate, Jean
l'Ecorcheur, who flays his captives alive."

There was nothing simulated, now, in the dead silence
that fell upon the crowd. The champing of the charger's
bit sounded loud and harsh in the interval of that awful
pause. It seemed a sentence of death, so stern was the
intelligence, and so crushing in its effects. It were as
though one of those avenging seers of old had descended
suddenly with a message from on high, and had proclaimed
" thus saith the Lord, set thine house in order, for thou shalt
die, and not live."

Bras-de-fer alone appeared utterly unconscious of the
heavy nature of the tidings he had brought. Springing
lightly from his selle, he gave his steed to one of his
esquires, and broke the spell, by crying, in a loud hearty
tone,—" To the ramparts, my merry men, to the ramparts,
an ye would not have this bloodsucker make a meal of us!"
And he was turning away, for the purpose of ascending the
flight of steps leading to the walls, when he was arrested by
the Abbot, who now, for the first time since the knight's
coming, found power to speak.

" Tarry awhile, Sir Bras-de-fer," said he, " for I would
fain question you. If it be sooth that the fiend l'Ecorcheur
(whom may God and St. Nicholas confound!"—here the

Abbot piously crossed himself) " be bound hitherward, and
seeks to lay his sacrilegious hands upon the patrimony of the
blessed Church, wherefore does it chance that her first
vassal, Sir Dreux de Barentin, rides to her defence with
such a scanty train? Is it possible that he comes alone, and
not, as of old, with banner displayed, and a goodly power of
bowmen, and spearmen, and with all the strength of carnal
war?"

" It is even so, my reverend friend," replied Sir Dreux,
or rather, as he was commonly called, Bras-de-fer, in-
differently, while his skilful eye took in at a glance all that
was passing with the troops posted above, " it is even so.
All my gathering consists but of myself, with Richard and
Anthony yonder, unless ye would count Bayard in the roll."

" False man, and false knight!" shouted the churchman,
who began to lose both patience and his senses, at once,
under this new shock, " I rede ye to know that St. Nicholas
can resume his grants; aye, and he shall do it. Did we not
give thee lands, wide and fair, to hold of the Abbey by
bridle and spear, and art thou not, as leal servant of the
Church, vowed to bring to her aid, whenever, and by
whomsoever, attacked, ten men-at-arms, each of them fully
equipped, and followed by two bowmen and a jackman?
Where be they, thou faithless vavasour? God and St.
Nicholas help us in our extremity, for, of a verity, we
perish, and there is none to succour us!"

During the first part of this speech, Bras-de-fer had been
leisurely scanning the military preparations, going on under
the ordering of William le Poer, and had evidently paid but
slight attention to the angry priest. But the tone of anguish

that marked the closing sentence touched him.   Kindly laying his hand on the Abbot's arm, he said to him, in a voice
of singular gentleness and feeling, " Pause, my good old
friend, ere you condemn me.   I must be brief, for I am
sadly wanted yonder, but the matter stands thus.   Last night,
when I received tidings of this pestilent invasion, I sent out,
as was my duty, to summon to my standard all,—and more
than all,—who were bound to bear arms in your defence.
By sunrise, this morning, the whole were reported, by my
muster-master, to be in waiting, and ready to set out.   But,
as untoward fortune would have it, the Lady Claude, my
wife, was taken with labour throes.   I could not move her
hither, nor could I leave her unguarded at home.   I did
what necessity compelled me to do.   To defend my castle
of Ennour, and her, I left my contingent, and surely it is a
feeble garrison enough, but hither I came myself, as bound
in honour, and in my devoir, to fight, and, if need be, to die
in your cause.   So courage, my dear Lord, we shall beat off
these routiers, stout knaves though they be, and with the
more credit, seeing the feebleness of our means of defence."

The Abbot groaned in spirit, most dismally.   " Ever have
I found," he sighed, " that a woman is at the bottom of all
evil or mischance.   For what saith a certain Father, ' Ubi
fœmina, ibi diabolus.'   And as for the glory of which you
speak, my fair son, would that in its place we had the two
score soldiers, who are now waiting the pleasure of the Lady
Claude."

" Sith it may not be mended, my Father," answered Bras-
de-fer, as he prepared to depart, " we must endure it as
well as we can, which is a piece of philosophy taught me

by old Froissart. Yet cheer up and fear not. I am no
braggart, God knows, still bethink thee that perchance my
arm and my leading may well balance, aye, and outweigh,
the services of a few hirelings. There are in Scilly scores of
such to be had for the buying, but there is only one Bras-
de-fer." So saying he ascended the steps, leading to the
outer rampart, and left the Abbot standing alone. The
latter felt the justice of his remark. Bras-de-fer, as a
leader, had a reputation of the highest order. His military
skill and judgment were unrivalled. Yet to lose the best
contingent of the house was mortifying enough.

"Surely" quoth the priest, "Sir Bras-de-fer hath reason
on his side. The best lance in merry England is worth a
score of common men. I would, however, that his fair wife
had chosen her time better. She is a woman, and it is ill
dealing with that troublesome sex. As old Sir John hath
it, we must remedy it as best we may." And the Abbot
walked slowly after Bras-de-fer, sorely vexed in spirit. But
the presence of his warlike vassal had inspired him with
something like confidence. He sought the ramparts, to
look around on what was passing, not indeed in a cheerful-
mood, but less downcast than before. So true it is that the
courage and high qualities of one man will often fill a host
of waverers with hope and alacrity, and infuse into their
bosoms the energy that is all his own.

No sooner had Bras-de-fer taken the command, than he
proved how correct was his estimate of his own value. All
the vassals capable of bearing arms were mustered, and
passed in review, and were then told off in divisions, each
of which was placed under the leadership of some veteran

soldier. The archers and cross-bow men were posted on the walls, which were both crenelated and machicolated, and preparations were made for pouring melted pitch, and boiling water, on the heads of the assailants, in case they should attempt a storm. The pontlevis was raised, and between it and the great gate, a wicket of which only was allowed to be open, there was constructed a semicircular embankment or breast-work, one end of which terminated at the wall, and the other joined the hill side. It was the height of a man's shoulders, and was defended by ten picked cross-bow men. It could only be approached in front, as the ground on the right was precipitous, and on the left the slope was swept and commanded by the great tower. The best and most disciplined of the whole array were drawn up in reserve, in the Abbey court. Having thus put everything in train, Bras-de-fer ordered a manchet of bread and beef, with a good black-jack of humming ale, to be served out to every man under arms: and then, cautioning all to be on their guard, and to quit themselves like men, and faithful children of the Church, he sought the Abbot, who was gazing fearfully abroad.

The scene that met their eyes was one of stirring interest, to a mere spectator, though, to those then looking upon it, it possessed a sterner and more terrible character. At the end of the wide slope before them, as it rose from the valley, under Bryher hill, was seen advancing, with some pretence to discipline, a vast body of men. They were marshalled in several divisions, each headed by its own leader. They consisted, as might have been expected, principally of foot, a few only being mounted on the small active horses called hobs, from which their riders in the military language of the time were called hobbilers or hobblers, and whence we also derive our name of cob. They were preceded by numbers of bowmen, who acted as scouts, and explored the ground. Generally speaking, their equipments were heterogeneous, and dimmed by use; but the experienced eye of Bras-de-fer remarked that the spear heads were bright and clean, from which he augured that, however rusty their defensive armour might be, their weapons of offence would be found service-able enough. In the rear of the several columns was beheld a mixed multitude, together with some captives, and a few carts charged already with plunder. At the head of the whole, clad in complete steel, rode the redoubtable l'Ecorcheur. He was followed by a man-at-arms, who filled the office of an esquire, and bore his lance. His arms were handsome, and his whole bearing that of one who affected some degree of state, either from vanity, or as a means of overawing others by that pomp and show, which always has its effect upon the multitude.

As soon as he had arrived within two bowshots of the Abbey, he halted his men, and drew them up in regular order, as well as the inequalities of the ground would allow. He then rode forward alone, taking care to keep out of the reach of an enemy's arrow. After making a careful survey of the place, he paused exactly opposite to that part of the walls, on which were the Abbot and Bras-de-fer. The latter, who had been watching his adversary's movements with great interest, came to the edge of the parapet, and stood there, erect and still, so that the whole of his gigantic proportions were visible to the besiegers. The two celebrated champions remained, for a time, face to face, neither of them speaking a word, and the eyes of all men being directed on them alone. Those, who were near to l'Ecorcheur, might behold a shade of disappointment and vexation cross his brow, but in no other way did he betray his annoyance, at finding himself thus confronted by one of the boldest warriors of the day. Bras-de-fer, on his part, looked with curiosity on the chief, whose name had become invested with so much unenviable notoriety. The silence that followed this reciprocal survey was first broken by the Reiter, who, advancing a few paces nearer to the Abbey, summoned it, loudly and peremptorily, to surrender.

"And what if we like it not, Sir l'Ecorcheur?" inquired Bras-de-fer.

"Death to every living soul within the walls," was the reply; "death to all alike, but, as you are the leader, a higher bough for your hanging."

"Gramercy for your courtesy, Sir Routier," said Bras-de-fer, "the walls of St. Nicholas are high, and his servants stout of heart, so we will strike a stroke in defence of holy Church, the more readily, too, since we like not to trust to your word, should we yield ourselves to your mercy, and crave grace. May it please you then, Sir Flayer, to retire out of arrow-flight, for if you remain longer where you are, we will try the temper of your corslet. Shoot, men, shoot! Arrows to the head! Shoot, trebuchet! St. Nicholas to the rescue, and set on!"

It was well at the moment, for l'Ecorcheur, that he took Bras-de-fer's advice. He escaped unharmed himself, but two arrows struck his charger, which bounded furiously, and nearly dismounted its rider. He became livid with passion, and gave orders instantly to commence the attack; while the manner, in which his commands were carried into effect, showed the defenders of the Abbey that they were dealing with no common foe.

A number of men first advanced, bearing before them those large pavoises, or pavises, which were used in opening approaches against a fortified place. These were shields, of about the soldier's height, and broad enough to cover him completely. Being of stout wickerwork, bound over with leather, they were sufficiently light to be manageable. Behind this shelter, which was borne by one man, followed an archer or cross-bow man, keeping himself protected from the hostile shot, and looking warily out for an opportunity of sending an arrow, or a bolt, at those who manned the walls. Several large vans, or moveable towers, which could be taken to pieces, or joined together, at pleasure, succeeded these; and, as soon as they were well posted, mangonels, and machines for throwing large stones, were brought forward. A sharp fire was maintained, without intermission, for nearly half-an-hour, at the end of which time there was a pause, as if by mutual consent. Both parties, as it were, drew off, to ascertain their respective damages, and to prepare for a fresh onset and defence.

The result of the inquiry was in favour of the Abbey. Not a man on the walls had been hurt. Two or three of the non-combatants, huddled together in the precincts and courts, had been slightly touched by spent shafts, but no serious casualty had occurred. On the side of the besiegers the list of wounded was far heavier. Nearly a dozen had

been killed or severely injured by the Abbey men, who shot
coolly from under cover. The bodies of the slain, and those
pierced by arrows, as they were carried, or as they staggered,
to the rear, were, in the eyes of both parties, an omen of
success or failure. The defenders were animated with hope
and courage, and the attacking forces were equally dispirited
and depressed.

Jean l'Ecorcheur himself, who was utterly unaccustomed
to reverses, actually foamed with rage. He was beside
himself. He shook his clenched fist at the Abbey, and
addressed its guardians with the foulest blasphemies. At the
same time he directed his men to begin the assault anew.
Long ladders were prepared, and brought to the front, while
a fresh band of archers came forward, and watched every
portion of the walls. While this was passing without,
Bras-de-fer was not idle within. His eye, and his over-
looking care, were everywhere. Amid a hail of arrows, he
seemed to bear a charmed life. Armed cap-à-pied, a bright
and lofty mark, he moved from post to post, advising some,
cautioning others, and speaking to all in that clear bold tone
of confidence, which a soldier loves. At last, he came to
the spot, where, sheltered by a corner tower, the Abbot
stood to watch the progress of the fray.

"What think you, Sir Bras-de-fer?" said he, as the
knight rejoined him, "how speeds the day with those sons
of Belial?"

"An' they succeed no better than hitherto" answered
the knight, "their's is but labour thrown away. Not a step
has been gained yet; but they have lost some of their best
men. Courage, my reverend friend, the Abbey of St.

Nicholas will be a virgin fortress still. But what is this?"
he added, pointing to a figure on the ramparts, at no great
distance from them. On a nearer approach, it was seen to
be the Abbot's favourite dwarf, dragging after him, with
difficulty, a weapon of antique form, and of enormous size
and weight. The sight seemed to rouse the Abbot's indignation and surprise to the highest pitch.

"Anathema maran-atha!" he cried, "the profane imp of
evil has laid his sacrilegious hands upon the feudal arbalete
of the blessed Monseigneur St. Nicholas, which he wrested
from the Cornish giant, who robbed Lombard merchants,
coming hither to traffic, and pious pilgrims, as they crossed
the Abbey lands; yea, and slew the heathen with his own
bow. Thou misshapen knave, knowest thou not the sanctity
of that consecrated weapon? Answer me, thou misbegotten
and mischievous varlet!"

"And knowest thou not, holy Lord Abbot," replied the
dwarf, "that a bolt from it hath pierced a coat of Spanish
mail, at five hundred good paces?"

With these words, much to the amusement of Bras-de-fer,
and to the wrath of the Abbot, he proceeded to drag his
load to the parapet, on which, with much trouble, he rested
it. He then attempted to string it, but in vain. The bow and
cord, alike of steel, resisted his efforts, and he chafed with
rage, at seeing himself thus foiled. Bras-de-fer walked to
his side, and watched him, as well as the weapon, with a
curious eye.

While this scene was passing within, the attack without
was recommenced, more hotly than ever. Jean l'Ecorcheur
stormed with fury, like a fiend. He rode in among the

pavoises, cursing and shouting to his men, who exerted themselves desperately, in hopes of gaining distinction under the eye of a leader, who never rewarded with a niggard hand. Their shot flew thick and fast, and wounded some of the besieged. At last he espied the Abbot in his place of safety. The sight of the good Priest seemed almost to drive him mad. He overwhelmed the Abbey, and all connected with it, with the vilest abuse. Raising himself in his stirrups, and shaking his mailed hand at the walls, he bade their defenders yield instantly, and be at his mercy.

"Thou dog of an Abbot!" he cried, "for the slaughter of my men, I will take with thee a reckoning, that shall deter others from following thy example. By all the fiends in hell, I will roast together, in a slow fire, thee, and the image of thy mock Saint, Nicholas, whom may Beelzebub "— the rest of the sentence was never spoken, for word passed not those brutal lips again.

Bras-de-fer, as was related above, stood by the dwarf, and watched his abortive efforts to bend the mighty bow of St. Nicholas. Suddenly, an idea seemed to strike him. Pushing the little man gently aside, he seized the string, and drew it to the spring, as lightly, as though it were a silken cord. Then he adjusted a bolt to the groove, and took a deliberate aim. And at the very moment when l'Ecorcheur was pouring forth his blasphemies against St. Nicholas, the bow of St. Nicholas avenged him. The bolt, entering his mouth, passed into his brain; and the routier, springing convulsively up into the air, fell upon the plain, a lifeless corse.

> "As it crashed through the brain of the infidel,
> Round he spun, and down he fell.
> Ere his very thought could pray,
> Unanealed he passed away,
> Without a hope from mercy's aid,
> To the last, a renegade."

"Well shot, quarrell," cried the exulting dwarf, but Bras-de-fer preserved a stern and thoughtful silence. He waved with his hand a signal for his men to cease their discharge, and then stood watching the effect of his blow.

That effect was, indeed, decisive. L'Ecorcheur, like Bras-de-fer, was a leader, who had no second to supply his place. At first there was a confused rush to the spot where his body lay, but when he was discovered to be past all aid, a panic fell on the great host, that had so lately obeyed him as one man, and it began to melt away, like the mists on a mountain-side. All the military train, with the plunder, was left standing. Before twilight came down, not a routier was in the island of Tresco. Their white sails gleamed upon the waves. The deliverance of the Abbey was complete.

Bras-de-fer, with the Priest, watched their rapid and disorderly retreat, along the margin of the broad lake, which then, as now, occupied the valley.

"Thine was a happy shot, Sir Knight," said the Abbot, "surely it was a blessed deed. St. Nicholas nerved thy arm, to smite that spoiler, hip and thigh. Thou hast slain the accursed Philistine, even while he railed against the servant of God."

"Sir Monk," replied Bras-de-fer, with unusual gravity, "I do not gainsay you, neither do I deny that the fall of Jean l'Ecorcheur, by my hand, has preserved your Abbey.

I cannot expect you to feel as a soldier feels. But this I
will say. He, whom men call the Flayer, routier as he was,
still was a valiant soldier. Truly, I slew him, and I did it
in a good cause. Yet he and I have ridden together under
the same banner, and fought in many a bloody field. It
would have pleased me better had we met, on yonder open
plain, horse to horse, and man to man, in fair and knightly
strife. As it is I smote him, after the fashion of the simple
dwarf, from under cover; as I have heard, in your holy
book, that Abimelech, a stout Jewish captain, was stricken
by the hand of a woman. Me seemeth it was not thus that
Bras-de-fer should have conquered in your cause."

"Tush, my son," said the Abbot, impatiently, "these be
silly questions of what is called honour. What matters it,
so long as the mad wolf be killed, by what hand, or by
what weapon, he falls?"

"True, Father," replied Bras-de-fer, "I believe you are
in the right. After all, our little friend here deserves more
credit than I. God inspired him with the idea, which I
put in practice. He conceived, and I only executed. Thus
God rebukes our pride, for He made Bras-de-fer second to
this feeble child. It is God alone who is our Deliverer.
To Him, and to His Name, be praise!"

CHAPTER X.

MENAVAWR, AND THE EASTERN ISLES.

 AIL, on a fine day, down New Grimsby channel, and you will enjoy a view as rugged, and as romantic, as any that you have hitherto found. Oliver's Castle is on your right, and above it is the grey ruin, bearing the name of the unhappy Martyr. As you gain the open sea, you will probably have a swell. The deep water generally heaves lazily, as if with a consciousness of its power, even when at rest. Sharks are not unfrequently met with here, and the air, especially in the breeding season, echoes with the cries of the numerous water-fowl, for which Scilly is so famous. Leaving Piper's-hole on the right, we steered towards Menavawr,* but the wash on the rocks was so heavy that we were unable to land. We contrived however to get on Round Island, and picked up a basket of cormorants' eggs. On the highest

---

* Commonly called after the usual English fashion "Man-of-war."

point of the island is a fine barrow and circle. The old sea-king has apparently not been left undisturbed in his solitary abode. Some idler, like myself, has turned aside to wrong the quiet of the dead. The puffin breeds, here, and at Menavawr, in great numbers, and we saw their parrot-like forms wheeling around us, as they watched our intrusion on their domain. The young cormorants were so tame that they fought each other before us, and would hardly get out of our way.

Leaving Round Island you cross St. Helen's pool, and reach the island of that name. Here there was once a church and, probably, a monastic establishment. Now it is utterly deserted. Some deer and goats were placed upon it a few years since, but only one of the former is left, and he goes backwards and forwards between this place and Tean. There are still standing the walls of the ancient pest-house.

We next visited Tean, or St. Theona, which is equally uninhabited, though at both there are walls and parts of buildings, some of the enclosures running far into the sea, and giving incontrovertible proof of the former union of many, if not all, of these now disjointed and separate rocks. Leland speaks of this portion of the group as especially dedicated to religion.—

"St. Lide's, whare of old was grate superstition."

Some think that St. Lide is a corruption of St. Elid, and that again another form of St. Helen.* Tean or Theona, which the erudite historian "much renowned for Greek" makes to be derived from that language, is now inhabited

---

* Others believe it to be Rat Island.

only by white rabbits, which are very beautiful, and remarkable for their long and silky fur. There is a Druidical circle on a hill called "Yellow carn." The whole place is very picturesque, and though its extent is but thirty-five acres, it consists entirely of hill and dale, and has many and charming views. We sailed from it, round St. Martin's, for the Eastern Isles. The sound is studded with rocks, terribly near the surface. A short time since a box was here washed up, bearing, I think, only the name of "Agnes Ewing." The vessel so called was a large Indiaman, that had left Liverpool for Calcutta. She was never heard of more, nor could any guess be made at her fate, save from this fragment, which was washed ashore at Tean. What a dread reply will be given when the trumpet shall sound, and the angel's voice go forth,—

"Give up thy dead, thou sea!"

As we passed through St. Helen's sound, I asked why the Parsonage, which faces the harbour, was built in a situation so exposed to a cold quarter. The reason was particularly Scillonian. Every one formerly smuggled here, and among others, the then clergyman. The cellars of the building are far larger than is necessary, for a very obvious reason, and the house was made to face the north-east, in order that the worthy incumbent might watch the shipping in the pool, and receive, and reply to, any signal. He was obliged to run away, from having been detected in some gross smuggling affair. His sister, who was as great an oddity as himself, died of starvation, though fifty pounds were found in her possession. At her funeral, the parson's cellar was unceremoniously invaded, and a scene ensued only to be

equalled at an Irish wake. Troutbeck the amusing historian
of Scilly, whose work is most interesting, left the islands, it
is said, from fear of the consequences of a similar offence.
In fact, I believe that had the Queen then lived at Scilly,
she would have smuggled, like other people.

Doubling St. Martin's, we enter Crow sound and steer
direct for the Eastern Isles. These are numerous, and, some
of them, large ; one, Great Ganilly, containing upwards of
sixteen acres. They are distinguished by various names, for
which, and for all local particulars, both here and elsewhere,
I must beg to refer to North's laborious and exact account,
as I only seek to record my impressions, and not the details,
of what I see. We landed on the Arthurs, there being three
of that name. On Great and Middle Arthur, are several
barrows, one very large and capable of containing many
persons. The remains of inclosures are visible, but there is
now nothing living but lop-eared rabbits and rats. Where
we embarked I fancied that I could trace the outline and
materials of an antique pier.* The walls too appeared to
be very old, almost, as it seemed to me, connected with the
circles and barrows. It is really painful to see these vestiges
of life and labour, like the dead bones spoken of by the
prophet, once instinct with life.

There is nothing remarkable in any of the other rocks,
except their picturesque roughness of form, and the fine
contrast of the surf, flashing over the blue deep, upon their

---

* I was not mistaken. A patriarch, nearly ninety years old, tells me
that this place was formerly called Arthur's quay ; and that, according to
ancient tradition, whenever one of its stones was by chance removed,
some invisible hand always replaced it by night.

grey stones and bright bays of sand. From them you emerge into the great ocean. The light-ship on the ridge called the Seven Stones is before you. On a clear day you can see the Land's-end, and you may lie in the stern of your boat, and muse about the Lionesse. The day is calm, a pair of sea-pies scream to you as you pass; so transparent is the water that, fathom deep beneath, you can distinguish rock from sand. All is repose, and beauty, and tranquillity. You are gliding by Arthur, and look upon its grey boulders. There, however, is a memorial of a different scene. Part of the mast of a large ship lies, broken and forgotten, on the shore. Why is it left there, unclaimed? Ask the tempest, ask the great green monster, over whose bosom you sweep, as it lies smiling and murmuring in the sunlight below!

CHAPTER XI.

TRESCO. No. 2.

HERE is in Tresco so much that is interesting and beautiful that it deserves a residence
of some days, to be devoted to exploring it.
Considering its very limited size, one is surprised at the variety of its scenery.   On
landing at the harbour, and passing the "Palace," * so
called from the place used for drying pilchards, as is usual
hereabouts, you ascend a slope, and reach the pretty little
Parsonage. From thence the view is lovely. Old Grimsby
harbour, and St. Helen's pool, lie below you, with Dolphin
Town, † and the neatly arranged church, and the excellent
schools. ‡ You are surprised at the appearance of all around
you. It is not picturesque alone, for the Island of Skye
could be that, with all its misery. It is not only retired and
undisturbed. It was so in the days of wreckers, when
parsons smuggled, and when guagers and duties were

---

* Not from an Inn of that name as North thinks.
† "Godolphin."
‡ Both the schools are very good.   The mistress of that for infants
teaches and manages them admirably.

unknown.   But there is everywhere an air of comfort, and
an aspect of content, which I never saw elsewhere.   The
fields are highly cultivated, the gardens are tended carefully,
the people are well dressed, and " there is not one poor man
in all their tribes."   Go into the little (quasi) cruciform
church.   You will see there, probably, as dense and as
attentive a congregation as you ever beheld.   Ask for a man
to do any service for you, and you will fail in procuring one,
for all are employed.   There is no Union here, for there are
no paupers to fill it.   In this thought is a charm greater
than that of the smiling prospect before our eyes, enchanting
though it be.   Read Woodley's account of these islands,
thirty years ago, and look at them now.   It is, under God,
the work of one English gentleman, accomplished in seventeen years, in spite of the Celtic spirit, and old inveterate
habits, and wrecks,* and the Duchy of Cornwall.

Crossing the downs to the left of the Parsonage, you
arrive at Charles's walls, consisting but of a few ruins, well
and boldly placed.   Below it is Cromwell's Castle, so called
according to the rule in Theodore Hook's song,—

> " And then he saved an Emperor, where
> No Emperor was near, Sir."

It is still kept in good order by the Board of Ordnance,
and, as it commands New Grimsby channel, would be useful
in beating off privateers, in time of war.   From hence round

---

* The very front of the gallery of the pretty church, at Tresco, is
formed of part of a wreck ; and the gallery itself, from a mere nautical
spirit of imitation, is placed so low, after the pattern of a ship's cabin, that
you must stoop in passing under it.   Most of the old houses in Scilly
have their rooms built like cabins, the ceilings being of wood, and not
more than six feet high.

the bluff to " Piper's-hole " is a very pleasant walk, and the
cave itself is well worth a visit. Preparation must be made
for it, by procuring a boat, in which to cross the pool within,
and by taking blue lights to burn,* when there. I wonder
what is the foundation of the tradition of the Piper, and his
wild music, dying away in the distance, until it is heard, and
he is seen, no more. Go where you will, you meet with
it. It resembles that tale of the traveller who set out in
a boat to explore the reservoir of a thousand columns, at
Constantinople, and who never returned. If it were but
true, what a life of agony might have been compressed in
those short hours! We are reminded of the person who
incautiously left his guide, in the imperial vault, at Vienna.
The rats are there seen, not by hundreds, but by millions.
His fate was only known by the sexton finding a few
scattered bones in a corner of the crypt, and some brass
buttons, which were recognised as having been his. These
dark scenes are terribly oppressive. Let us come out into
the open air, and leave the ghost of the Piper in his funeral
cave. God's sun-light is glimmering over the calm sea,
that breaks, in low, solemn music, upon the rocks at our feet.

Listen, for a moment, to a tale of the civil wars, connected
with that shattered peel above, and with this dismal subterranean vault below. The incidents mentioned in it took
place principally here. We will therefore call it—

A LEGEND OF " PIPER'S-HOLE."

---

* This must be done cautiously. Some sappers and miners lately
kindled a fire in the cave, and were in great danger. One of the party
was carried out insensible.

A LEGEND OF "PIPER'S-HOLE."

IN the spring of 1651, there was sorrow and confusion of face at Scilly. Blake and Ayscough, the rebel leaders, were approaching with the sea and land forces of the Parliament, to wrest the Islands from the gallant Sir John Grenville, the kinsman of that Bevill Grenville, who died so nobly for his king, on Lansdowne heath. The remains of the royal army, composed chiefly of officers, and gentlemen of blood, prepared to meet the storm, which they did not hope to resist with success. Had they been, like their enemies, men who preferred their own selfish interests to those of their country, they would have treated with Van Tromp, who made them the most tempting offers, on condition of their ceding the islands to him. But the Cavaliers knew that their duty was to contend against treason, not to imitate it. They refused even to listen to his proposals, or to convey to the stranger any portion of the old realm of England. They looked forward to the last act of that long agony, ready to meet, face to face, a superior force,—ready, if need be, to die in harness, or, if doomed to be survivors of that dreadful ordeal, ready to endure to the end, to go forth from a country where they could no longer find it in their hearts to abide, and to bear their honourable scars to a land in which they could dwell, until, in the expressive language of Scripture, " this tyranny be over-past."

It was in Tresco, as it then began to be called, that the swords of the opposing parties first crossed each other. We well know how many causes had combined to add bitterness to the ordinary fierceness of war. The Puritan, and the Cavalier, not only waged a religious strife, and felt a religious hatred; they had not alone the exasperation of personal motives, of wrong and injury on the one side, and of contempt and loathing on the other, to sting and to urge them on, but there was in both a spirit yet darker and more ruthless than these. Those who murdered the " man Charles Stuart" were likely to show scant mercy to the malignants, who wore upon their bosoms a likeness * or a bloody relic of the Martyred King. So, with these feelings, both parties made their dispositions for the coming shock. And as Tresco was the first object of attack, Sir John Grenville employed all the means at his disposal to put it into a respectable state of defence.

It was protected by a fort, situated on the heights above New Grimsby, and called "Charles's Castle." The principal garrison of the Royalists was there. But the ancient

---

* One of these is in the possession of my family. It was worn by my ancestor, Sir Ralph Whitfeld, of Whitfeld, a faithful servant and minister of King Charles, and is a beautiful miniature of the Martyr, with the axe on the reverse.

Abbey of St. Nicholas was also intrenched and fortified ; and
batteries were established on all the commanding positions
round the coast. There was no lack of volunteers in such
a cause. A band of fiery youths, " the full of hope, misnamed forlorn," watched the approach of the hostile fleet ;
and many a bold passage of arms seemed destined to take
place, and many a desperate encounter to occur, ere Tresco
should be lost and won.

The command of the whole place was entrusted to a young
gentleman, named William Edgcumb, of a noble house in
the West of England. His years, indeed, were not many ;
but those were times when capacity for service was not
measured by years. In those trying and terrible days, the
boldest and the worthiest came out, involuntarily, from the
common herd, and took the lofty place assigned to them,
as the nobility of intellect and of mind. The instinct of
Heaven's patent was recognized at once ; and many a young
man, like Graham of Montrose, passed over the heads of
white-haired veterans, and was cheerfully followed and
obeyed. So was it in this instance. William Edgcumb
was but a child, when, a few years before, he had left his
home in Devonshire to draw for King Charles a sword
almost too weighty for his arm. Since then, he had ridden
over well-nigh every field fought between the two parties,
and had gained experience, and won distinction, in all. And
now, a youth in age, but a leader of high and approved
qualities, he was placed, by Sir John Grenville, in the post
of honour, and of danger, at Tresco. He was selected to
meet the first onset of those bands, whose iron discipline
had stemmed, and rendered vain, the dashing and devoted

bravery of the cavaliers. The task assigned to him was
hopeless. The might of the Protectorate, which had stricken
down the crown of England, was not to be checked by a
handful of zealous men, on a distant and rocky isle. There
was no prospect of success. But though there was no chance
of victory, there was, on the other hand, a certainty of that
which is equally dear to a proud and a faithful heart. There
was honour to be gained; there was duty to be done; there
were dangers to be met; there was vengeance to be gratified.
And above all, to one who reverenced his murdered sovereign,
and clung to the cause of his party and his house, there was
to be sought that distinction, which attaches itself always to
the leader amid high deeds, when those he loves look on
admiringly, and those he hates stand before him, face to face.
With these inducements to play his part worthily, William
Edgcumb had taken the chief command at Tresco, and
prepared to hold it to the last.

He did hold it, as he had vowed to do, on the true faith
of a cavalier. The enemy first effected his landing in front
of the Abbey, which he attacked in force, and carried by
storm. The relics of the garrison were rallied by William
Edgcumb in person, who collected all the parties holding
different detached posts, and fell so fiercely on the rebels,
and maintained a fight so long and so doubtful, that he was
on the point of recovering the Abbey itself. In the midst
of the bloody contest, when success hung on the balance,
the building took fire, and was soon in a blaze. William
Edgcumb sullenly withdrew his men, and fell back upon his
last stronghold, the ancient castle, named after his honoured
master, Charles. There he organised his means of defence,

and prepared, proudly and silently, for the last closing scene. The shock was not long in coming, and, when it came, it was irresistible. Blake in person brought his ships into New Grimsby, and directed their fire upon the position of the Royalists. On the land side the attack was conducted by Colonel Fleetwood, a stout and tried soldier. The strife was stubborn, but its conclusion was such as might have been anticipated, from the inequality of the contending parties. The fortress was captured by a sudden and desperate assault. When the rebel forces were fairly in possession of the place, and the day was evidently lost, the Governor, faithful to his charge, disdained to surrender, or to accept the honourable terms offered by Fleetwood. He descended to the magazine, laid a train of powder on the ground, took a pistol from his belt, and coolly exclaiming "God save King Charles!" pulled the trigger, and essayed to bury the old fortalice, with its mingled crowd of true men and traitors, in one common ruin. The earth shook as with an earthquake. There was a breathless lull, after that torrent of flame, and then men looked in each other's faces, with a mute inquiry of horror and dismay. When these feelings had in some degree subsided, and measures could be taken for restoring order, and for retaining what had been so fearfully won, it was found that though the roof was blown off, the walls were comparatively uninjured. Some hasty repairs were therefore effected in the breaches, caused by the previous attacks; two hundred Parliamentarians were quartered within the place, under the command of Colonel Fleetwood; and, finally, the dead were gathered together, to be buried in a soldier's grave. It was, however, remarked that the body of the

Governor was not found, after the closest search. A flag of truce, on the part of Sir John Grenville, from St. Mary's, had come to demand it, for interment. The young cavalier was dear to his general, and to his comrades, and all ranks were anxious to pay the last honours to one whom all repected and loved. But their wish was ungratified.

They doubted not that he had perished with so many others, by his own devoted act. They sought for him sorrowing, but they found him not. Every facility was given to their inquiries, but to the strictest investigation there was only one result. They found him not.

In a couple of days matters resumed their usual course at Tresco. The island being wholly occupied by the forces of the Commonwealth, only the usual military precautions were taken, and people went about their ordinary business, as before. The inhabitants were attached to the Royal cause, and loved little the steeple hats, and grotesque manners of the new comers. They dared not show these feelings, save by tacit dislike, and by avoiding, as much as they possibly could, all intercourse with the rebels. It is said that, at Scilly, women govern the men, and, in this case, it was the gentler sex that took the lead in manifesting their aversion to the Puritans. There could not, indeed, be a stronger contrast between two classes of men sprung on the same soil, than existed betwixt the sour Independents, with their grimaces, and their cant, and those high-born and graceful youths, whose very failings of gallantry, and reckless profusion, only endeared them to the Scillonian damsels. So there arose between the conquerors and the conquered that silent war, which is so galling, and so difficult withal to be conducted with success. The soldiers of the Lord, as they styled themselves, found their claims held very cheap among the Delilahs of Tresco. Their most unctuous compliments, and tenderest snuffles, only excited contempt or ridicule. So the Puritans confined themselves to their quarters, singing there their psalms out of tune their own way, and devoting the Moabitish maidens to Satan, whose children, the cavaliers, they were so ill-advised as to prefer to the saints and lights of Israel.

There was one exception to the general character of the victors. The young daughter of Colonel Fleetwood had accompanied the expedition, and had joined her father at the fort, after its storm and capture. She had no mother, for the Colonel had been early left a widower, so that her home was with him. Most men have a weak point in their hearts, and that of Colonel Fleetwood was excessive fondness for his child. The love he had borne to her mother was transferred, and strengthened by its transference, to the only pledge that love had given him. Nor was the object of that beautiful idolatry unworthy of it. She was very fair, with a broad brow of modest intelligence, and an arch spirit in her hazel eye that somewhat protested against her starched wimple, and the discreet amplitude of fold, in which a godly maiden then wrapt her charms from profane eyes. She was romantic, too, like most of the lovely and the young, and was not prevented from indulging in her tastes by her doting father. He was, perhaps, fonder of her from the very difference that existed between her habits and his own. The ascetic gloom of his personal and party manners could not withstand the sunshine which her face threw upon his

path. He had not the heart to cloud it by severity or
rebuke. Many there were, of those zealous for the Lord,
who thought the damsel no better than one of the Babylonian
sisterhood, or as one of those daughters of men, who seduced
the sons of God to sin. They predicted evil of her, as with
her gay laugh, and merry jest, she wandered abroad, even
where she listed. Nay, they resented either her levity, or
her scoffs, so openly and so warmly, as to take up their
parable against the stout old Colonel, and to make sundry
unsavoury comparisons between his daughter, and a lady
who delights in scarlet robes. One Habakkuk Plead-with-
the-Lord counselled his hearers, in a sermon especially
directed to this subject, to make known their sentiments
before the congregation; which piece of advice, being carried
into effect rather incautiously, was construed into mutiny by
the Colonel, who incontinently hung the Rev. Mr. Plead-
with-the-Lord, and five of his audience, on the rock, since,
from their fate, called "Hangman's isle." And thenceforth
the fair Mildred Fleetwood was suffered to range alone over
the downs and carns, sitting, and dreaming away many
an hour, with her eyes fixed upon the sea, and her heart,
perchance, lost in its aimless search for that love which is
the sole object of a woman's existence.

She was once thus occupied, yearning, unconsciously,
after the unknown, and, peradventure, the unattainable, and
resting, lost in these musings, amid the wildest portion of
the belt of rocks, which girds in all that side of Tresco.
The time was suited to the spirit of the place, and of her
who visited it, for the summer eve was just melting into
twilight, and the sea below lay slumbering in a waveless

calm. She had descended a steep ledge of granite, and was seated in a little cove, near the mouth of an ancient cavern, called "Piper's-hole." It had an evil reputation in the neighbourhood. It had taken its name from some mysterious tale of death, connected with one who had penetrated too far into its labyrinths, and who had never returned. It was said, indeed, to pass under the sea, and to join a cave of the same name, near Peninnis head, in St. Mary's. The common people shunned it, with superstitious awe. At that period, no one doubted that phantoms were permitted to appear on earth, and tales of possession and of witchcraft were circulated as articles of faith. The most learned and most religious men were not exempt from this weakness, as good old Richard Baxter's book abundantly testifies. So "Piper's-hole" enjoyed and maintained its supremacy of ghostly visitations. Nor was this belief confined to the studious or to the weak. It was held also by those who were counted the first soldiers in Europe. A Puritan sentinel, placed here on out-post duty, averred that he saw, issuing from the bosom of the earth, a grim figure clothed in white, that shook its finger at him with a menacing gesture, and so frightened him, that he fell flat upon his face, and when he regained his senses, the ghastly form was gone. Little, however, recked fair Mildred Fleetwood of these tales of horror. Perhaps they were even not displeasing to her. They gave food to her morbid appetite for novelty. They excited her romantic feelings. So, as was often her wont, she strayed to the haunted spot, and there sate, in her musing mood, thinking how fair were all the objects around, and being, unconsciously, herself the fairest there.

A sudden noise, as it seemed, close to her, made her start and turn round. She saw, almost at her side, that which, perhaps, would possess no terrors for a maiden's heart, and which yet was more dangerous to her tranquillity than all the phantoms from the tomb.

There stood by her the figure of a young man, whose appearance pleaded eloquently in his favour, even though he spake not a word, for his handsome features were pale and wasted, and his frame seemed bowed down with pain and feebleness. In his whole bearing and manner was the unmistakeable impress of gentle blood. His brow was bound round with a scarf, as if to cover a wound; his attire was, though rich, torn and stained; and his figure was bent, and full of weakness, and lassitude. Mildred Fleetwood gazed on him with timid and speechless surprise. There are some men whom women instinctively trust, and the stranger was one of these. She looked upon him, then, with astonishment, but without a particle of fear. Puritan as she was, she was a lady by birth, and felt a somewhat ungodly pride in the six martlets of her father's shield. She knew, intuitively, that she was in the presence of a gentleman, and she trusted in his claims, and in her own. The unknown spoke first, and addressed her thus :—

"Fair lady, whose features bely that vile garb, who are you, and how is it that you do not fear to approach this haunted spot, from which the very boldest shudder and turn away?"

"I am Mildred Fleetwood," replied she timidly, "why should I, having done no evil, and meaning none, dread to venture here? But you, whence do you come, and why are you in this place, and where is your abode?"

The young man looked at her for a moment, thoughtfully, and his face assumed by degrees a gentler, and even a tenderer expression. Still he did not speak, until, emboldened by his silence, she repeated the last question, when he replied to her simply,—

" If you have courage, come and see."

He held out to her his hand. After a moment's hesitation, the love of the marvellous, and womanly curiosity, and, perhaps, a rising feeling of pity and of partiality, prevailed. She took the hand extended to her, and, supported by her guide, advanced towards the mouth of Piper's-hole.

It were difficult to describe her sensations, as they proceeded in silence towards the cavern of ill repute. They were not exactly fearful, but more like a thrill of absorbing interest, mingled with romance, and with a strange trust in her pale and graceful guide. They moved slowly, until they reached the low-browed entrance of the vault, when the youth entreated her courteously, and with a respect befitting one who addressed a Queen, to pause, while he went on alone. He apparently kindled a torch, for a quick light streamed up in the dim chasm, and gilded his form as he returned. He again took her hand, and invited her onward, and she once more complied. Stooping low at intervals, they passed the rude portals of the cavern, and found themselves within its precincts. Few there were, at that epoch, who would not have feared to tread the pavement of that dread spot, as night was falling around. But, sooth to say, the courage of a young maiden will dare many perils, especially with one whom she trusts sharing those perils by her side.

It was a place to charm and fascinate a lover of Nature. The cave rose to a lofty height, growing higher as they proceeded, and terminating, as it appeared, at a distance of about fifty paces, in a dark and fathomless pool, on which floated a small boat.

"You have done much, lady," said the youth, when they reached it, "will you now turn back, or even venture on, and solve the mystery of Piper's-hole?"

He offered his arm, to assist her in entering the skiff, and, after a natural pause, and a momentary tremor, she rested on it, and stepped over the side. A few strokes of an oar sent the little vessel flying along the dim pool, and it soon grounded on the sand at the opposite extremity. Leaping lightly on the shore, he went forward, and again kindled a torch, which he brought with him in his hand, and held down to guide her steps, as she disembarked and followed him. She found herself in a vaulted room, of considerable extent, bounded on three sides by the solid rock, and on the fourth by that black lake, which had just borne them thither. In one corner was a bed, covered with a soldier's cloak. Some arms lay beside it, and there were scattered around many boxes, and packages of various sizes; and some provisions were seen in an open basket, by the head of the conch. All these things Mildred Fleetwood took in, woman-like, at a glance. She then turned, and gazed earnestly upon her mysterious companion. He smiled at her look of inquiry, and said, in a gentle voice, such as a woman loves to hear, for it is the tribute of strength to her weakness,—

" Well, lady, you have learned the secret of my abode, and you have a right to know the rest. You have told me your name, and I will requite your confidence by entrusting you with mine. Yet it must sound strangely in the ears of your father's daughter. I am William Edgcumb."

The fair Puritan started, but not with fear. It was, indeed, the famous leader of the Royalists, so long deemed dead, and so sincerely mourned, who now stood beside her, in that solitary cave. The tale of his escape from death was soon told. He had been flung to a considerable distance by the explosion that destroyed the fortress, but, after a long swoon, had recovered to find himself, though bruised and weak, almost without a wound. In the confusion that followed the capture of the place, he had managed to crawl away unseen, favoured by the shadows of evening, and had gained Piper's-hole, which had been formerly used, under his directions, as a hiding-place for stores. There he had remained, awaiting an opportunity of escape from the island, and subsisting partly on what had been placed there by his orders, and partly on food conveyed to him by a fisherman whom he had employed, and to whom he had confided the place of his retreat. They had contrived, and put into practice, the little spectral delusions, which, coupled with the bad reputation of the locality, had served to drive away all intruders from the spot, until Mildred Fleetwood had ventured there. These things were told, in a manner that went to the maiden's heart. She listened, and pitied, and looked wistfully upon the face of him who had done high deeds, but spake of them so modestly, and there was a tear in her eye when she parted from him, as he prayed her that she would meet him yet once more; and she went not without a low whispered promise to return.

She came again, according to her pledge, and many were the long hours spent in sweet communings within that cavern; and many a vow of constancy was given and received; and, as his eye regained its fire, and his step its buoyancy, her brow began to grow thoughtful, and her soft cheek waxed pale. At last, one evening, at the trysting place, he informed her of the arrival of that hour which she had so much dreaded. A boat was even then in readiness to take him, in the disguise of a fisherman, past the cruisers of the rebels, to St. Mary's. He pressed her to fly with him, and to become his bride. The struggle between love and duty in her heart was a sore one, her bosom swelled almost to bursting, and her brain burned, but if, for a second, she wavered, it was but for a second only. She steadily refused to fly. She was trusted, loved, idolized, by her father. He was alone in his old age. His life was centred in her. It broke her heart to part from her lover, but she knew that it would break her parent's heart to part from her, and her choice was made. She bade her lover God-speed, and charged him to remember her, and to expect happier times. It was now her turn to soothe and to support him. The tender girl became the comforter of the high-born and high-spirited man. He felt the justice of her pleading, and acquiesced in her decision, though man's innate selfishness could not but chafe against it. Finally, they parted, after a long embrace. He went, to suffer for his faith, in exile; and she remained, to return, day after day, to the scene of her vanished happiness, and to pray for him who was afar off, and who, by being faithful to his God, and to his King, gave an earnest of his fidelity to her.

Years passed by, long weary years, for them both. At intervals, few and far between, they had communicated with each other, but they had no hope of meeting, until the shadow of the Protectorate fleeted away, amid derision and contempt, and Charles the Second was restored. Then, indeed, a change came over their fortunes. Honoured and trusted by the Monarch, William Edgcumb returned in his train to England. He had no difficulty in protecting Colonel Fleetwood, who was permitted to retire to his estate in Buckinghamshire, and there end his days in peace and tranquillity. His old antagonist, and present benefactor, became his son-in-law, and he lived to see around his hearth children sprung from that mixture of loyal and republican blood. He ceased even to wonder at the change in his own sentiments, when he felt more inclined to smile than to shake his head at the romantic adventure of Piper's-hole. And his eye actually lightened with pleasure, when he heard that, among the beauties of the Court, one of the fairest, the merriest, and the most virtuous, was the daughter of the old Puritan officer, Mildred Edgcumb.

CHAPTER XII.

TRESCO. No. 3.

THE dim sepulchral cave looks positively brighter for the scene shadowed forth in it by fancy. You turn away from it with regret, and advance to the edge of that rocky barrier, against which the sea plays and whispers, coying it in each tiny cove, and around each fantastic outwork of Nature's planting, making low sweet music everywhere, and pausing awhile timidly, ere it retires, and sinks back again into repose.

Facing you are Menavawr and Round Island, from the top of which latter a Druidical barrow looks down upon you. Before you rolls the same ocean, which bore hither the barks of old, when the prophet wrote of those that came from Edom, with dyed garments from Bozrah,—that is, in the vernacular, Byrsa, or Carthage, a Phœnician colony. On the height, to your left, is the solitary ruin of King Charles. It should be touched with a gentle hand, for Scilly was the last place in the realm of England that upheld his cause. What volumes could be compiled out of the history of those devoted men, who, from all quarters, gathered together here, for a last stubborn stand! They were, truly, the children

of the captivity, enduring loyally unto the end. Lady
Fanshawe's account of the place, at that period, with her
half sorrowful, half whimsical, privations and sacrifices, is
highly interesting. All this rambling and disjointed musing
floats through your brain, as for a moment you stand and
look around. It is difficult to check the imagination, when
thus let free into the shadowy regions of the past. There
is the Phœnician, loosely draped in his graceful robe, with
its carved fibula; there is the Dane, looking from his tomb,
among the eyries yonder; and the Briton with his torques
and the mystic medal upon his breast; and the fair-haired
Saxon, gazing upon some inspired Prophetess; and the
awful Roman; and the gay Cavalier, faithful to death, and
singing to his mistress,—

> " Yet this inconstancy is such
>   As thou, too, shalt adore;
> I could not love thee, dear, so much,
>   Loved I not honour more."

and the sullen Puritan, half hypocrite and half fanatic—and
then the dim procession disappears, and there is nothing left
but the measured diapason of the deep, and the scream of
the wild bird, as it flits by, and, everywhere around, Nature
in all her majesty!

By following the coast, you arrive at Dolphin Town again,
and pass Permellin carn, and Merchants' rock, and get a
fine view of St. Helen's, and of Tean. On reaching the
north-eastern side of the island, you gain Pentle bay, beyond
which are some very picturesque masses of rocks, and an
imperfect circle or barrow. The northern promontory of
Pentle bay is called Lizard point. From all these carns
there is a striking panorama of St. Mary's pool, and Hugh

Town, and St. Agnes, which to-day is shrouded in mist, and appears larger and more distant than it really is.

We have now made the circuit of Tresco, and are about to return to our boat. The Abbey lies before us, with its romantic grounds, through which we are kindly permitted to pass. I had made up my mind to say nothing about the Abbey gardens. Englishmen have, in general, a distaste for any one who goes about "taking notes," even if he does not "print them." I sent the first chapter on Tresco to the press, and kept silence, but it was indeed pain and grief to me, and I could refrain no longer. I should wrong the sense of beauty, which is a part of man's divine inheritance, were I, by my apparent indifference, to seem insensible to the combination of sweet and lovely things, effected, in that spot, by the magic of art, of Nature carefully developed, and of the most exquisite taste. Still any mere description would be unmeaning and vain. Tea and coffee plants, the pepper and the arundo donax of the West Indies, the phormium tenax of New Zealand, the brugmansia of Chili, oranges, aloes, lilies from Japan, geranium-hedges from twelve to fifteen feet high, the graceful clianthus, like a waste parasite, crassulaceæ in vast masses, a hundred varieties of mesembrianthema in one group, growing in the open air, without protection, throughout the year.—What do these words offer to the mind ? They cannot give

"The charm that speaks, the music of the eye;"

nor can they convey the remotest idea of that glorious and glowing reality, the like of which I never saw before, and which I can never hope to behold again.

On our way through these marvellous temptations, we

pause for a moment to look at some magnificent specimens of mesembrianthema, covering the angle of rock, formed by the stones of a quarry. A group of workmen is busily excavating the hill-side. While we admire the flowers, one of the labourers gives a cry of surprise, and the others hurry to the spot. He has broken into what appears a vault, formed of smooth flat stones. A few more strokes of the pickaxe enlarge the aperture, and lay bare its contents. Some faded relics of mortality are taken carefully from what was fondly deemed their last retreat. They suggest the following tale, which will fitly close the account of our pleasant visit to Tresco.

THE DANE'S GRAVE.

AD were the days, and bloody, that fell upon merrie England, at the close of the tenth century. The race of Alfred had degenerated and dwindled away. Its feeble sceptre had passed into the nervous grasp of a Danish rover, Canute the Great. Nor was his title to supreme power undeserved. His dooms, or laws, were but a restoration of the old Saxon ordinances, telling us, by their mild and gentle spirit, the secret of their author's successful usurpation of the throne. Were it not for his "Charta de Forestâ," the authenticity of which we cannot doubt, we find in his statutes nothing which a legislator of the present time might not adopt. But the soul of a Northern Nimrod breathes in that awful sentence,—"Si nobilis cervum in regiâ forestâ occiderit, nobilitate careat; si liber, libertate; si servus, *corio*." *

Yet firm and paternal as were the character and the government of the new dynasty, the state of England, of

---

* "If a noble shall have killed a stag in the royal forest, let him be deprived of his nobility; if a freeman, of his freedom; if a serf, of his skin!"

the neighbouring coasts, and of its seas, was dark and melancholy. Upon the province of Neustria the Northmen had come down in a black swarm, and had given it the name* of those stern settlers. The Saxon Witan had confirmed the throne to the conqueror, and his followers had found a resting-place in many parts of England, especially in the kingdom of Northumbria. Yet the children of the North were not yet satisfied with plunder. The sea sent forth its rovers, pillaging and dealing in massacre against every one, but chiefly against the holy men who dwelt in monasteries. The monks of Chester long told of the fearful inroad from which they then suffered. Everywhere there was terror, and desolation, and death. Balefires were lighted on each headland, whenever the raven standard was descried. At the first glimmer of their ominous warning, men took bill and bow, the church bells tolled for glaas, and from lip to lip flew the news, "It is the Dane, the Dane!" Among those martial wanderers none was more dreaded, nor more terrible than the fiercest of the Vikingir, the young Berserker of the North, Ulf, of the blood of Thor.

He was no mean pirate. Fame, and not plunder, was his object. He struck heavily and often, but it was at the mighty, not the lowly and defenceless, that he aimed his blow. Yet there was an exception to this lofty rule. He hated, with the intensity ever inspired by a religious difference, the monks and nuns of Christendom. Wherever he went, he consigned their hallowed dwellings to the flames. He smote and spared not. And there were many places of this

---

* Normandy.

sort, easily assailable, upon the shores, or on the islands, of
the Anglian seas. Especially had he wreaked his wrath
on the Sorlings, or Scilly; not then, as now, a cluster of
mere islets, but one great main land, covered with a dense
population, and possessing several religious establishments.
Around the soft climate, and rich shores, of the devoted
spot, Ulf, the Dane, loved to linger. He burned the church
of St. Helen's, and surprised and sacked the ancient shrine
of St. Lide's, and laid waste the little tabernacle of St.
Theona. The isle of Ennour was too strong to fear the
attack of any rover, and the fair Abbey of Iniscaw defied
his efforts. Several times he endeavoured to take it by
stratagem, but the pious monks kept that committed to their
charge, and held him at bay. At that time, members of the
religious orders were less scrupulous about bearing arms
than they became in other and safer days. The Saxon
recluse drew an arrow to the head, and donned a casque,
and wielded sword and brownbill in defence of his dwelling
and of his life.* So when Ulf threatened the Abbey, ere
its vassals could be gathered together for its protection,
Leofric himself, the good Abbot, put on armour of proof,
and superintended the defence. Woe to the nithering, the
dastard, who shrunk from his duty then. His penance was
to sit upon the stone floor, and to dine with the animals, after
even the serfs had finished. But neither obedientiarius, nor

---

* This account of the military spirit of the Saxon monks is by no
means overcharged. Before the Conquest, both Bishop and Abbot often
rode in harness. Any reference to the chronicles of those times will
confirm this statement. Froissart's Bishop of Norwich, so late as the
fourteenth century, is well known.

novice, had ever thus been slack in danger. All knew the peril, and all met it like sons of Hengist and of Horsa. There was an hereditary antipathy between the two races that needed no violence to stimulate it into action. The brave Leofric set an example that was cheerfully followed. The meanest thrall of the convent would have scorned to hold back, even could he, by his remissness, hear those magical words, "Theow and esne be thou no longer, but go forth folk-free," and stand up a man. It may be supposed from this recital that the feelings of Ulf the Viking towards the Abbey and the brethren of Iniscaw, or Tresco, were anything but friendly. They were, in fact, exasperated by frequent failure and slight defeat. He lay off the shore, unwilling to leave it, and yet unable to get anything by remaining. All the stores and stock were collected together in places of safety. If he landed to hunt the wild boars, then numerous in the alder-brakes, from which this part of the main land derived its name* (Iniscaw meaning the Isle of Elders), he was liable to sudden onslaughts from the thanes and franklins who supported the Abbey. And even the monks and their men-at-arms, as he passed their walls, skirmished with him ; and once, as he went across the causeway that spanned, and still spans, the Abbey pool, they took him at a disadvantage, and encountered him so home, in the narrow passage, where numbers were of no avail, that he was driven into the lake, and would have been slain or taken, had not a reinforcement from the ships come up and rescued him.

---

* Perhaps, for there are two derivations.

Judge ye, therefore, if there were not bitterness of heart between the Fathers and Ulf the invincible.   He was, for the first time, checked, and checked by an adversary in his eyes the most hateful and the most despicable.   He, like a true Dane, quaffed deep draughts of mead, and metheglin, and hydromel, and uttered threats of vengeance, and planned new attempts, in all of which he failed.   No sooner had he landed in force, than the cresset-beacon on the great tower blazed up, and was answered from the strong castle of Ennour, and from the places where watch and ward were kept by vassal, and vavasour ; and the light of spearheads and helmets glinted from every brow, till Ulf was compelled to go back sullenly, and re-embark.   So passed the time, until the bravest of the Vikingir was like to be foiled by a cowl, and to sail back, bootless and laggard, unto his own land.

At length fortune threw in his way a chance of success, even when his prospects seemed desperate. Leofric, Abbot of St. Nicholas, was a high-spirited and choleric man, holding the rover cheap, and laughing to scorn his threats.   The Monk had been a soldier in his youth, and still felt a kindred sympathy with chain-mail and a trusty brand.   It was he who had driven back, in the melée, the fierce Ulf, and had well nigh mastered his sword.   So if the unchristened Dane fumed and fretted against the Shavelings, ye may suppose that the stout Priest railed at the lurdane,* as it was then the fashion to term the Scandinavian buccaneers, and held it foul scorn to be cooped up in his walls by a rover of the sea.   The feeling of bravado and of defiance soon became

---

* *Quasi*, Lord-Dane.

irresistible. One day the Abbot looked abroad over the fair
lands of Iniscaw. The sun lay like molten silver upon their
bosom. In the valleys, and amid the brakes, soft shadows
floated, like spirits brooding in a moment of repose over the
earth. Near the shore the gay galleys of Ulf rested upon
their shadows, seeming so innocent, and yet, like many a
beautiful deceit, full of peril. The Abbot frowned as he
gazed. "Son of a sea wolf," he muttered, " thou shalt no
longer coop me up within my walls on a day so heavenly!
Bid the lay servitors saddle my palfrey, and unleash the
brachs; we will forth to hunt a boar, if all the demons of
Valhalla were in our way! Thou, Alfgar the cellarer, shalt
be my squire of the body, and thou, young Edwin my
cnicht.* Arm, my children, and to horse ! "

The reckless spirit of the impetuous churchman ran, like
an electric shock, through the bosoms of his train. Soon
they bouned them for the chase. Wild boars then roamed
through the woods of Scilly, and so did the grey wolf. Even
in the time of Leland, the former were numerous at Tresco.
So, well practised at the sport, and tired of their long
confinement, the garrison, and many of the monks of St.
Nicholas, sallied forth from the great gates. They were a
gallant train. Athelstan, the conqueror, had scarcely ridden
with more bravery, when he wrested these lordships from
the Pagans, and bestowed them upon the Church. Perhaps
with their domains they had inherited from him their love of
sylvan sports, for which, indeed, the country of Cornwall
has always been celebrated, since Tristram invented his

---

* The word *cnicht* was equivalent to youth.

famous mot upon the horn, and hunted in the greenwood.
They went forth gaily, taking no heed of the raven that flew
so near them, and who watched their progress, as the caval-
cade wound round the head of the lake, and disappeared.

Their course was apparently pleasant and secure. The
day was spent in their unwonted enjoyment, and it was
evening ere they returned, bringing with them a huge boar,
slain by the hand of the Abbot himself. They reached,
without interruption, the little pier at the lower town, and
were passing the brakes that clothed that extremity of the
Abbey hill, when their progress was rudely barred. A flight
of arrows drove back the ceorls and cnichts, who formed
the advance. As they turned and fled, from every quarter
arose a shout, of whose terrible import none was ignorant,
"Ulf to the charge! Ulf for the Raven Standard!" And on
came the ferocious invaders, and at their head was Ulf,
brandishing his spear, and looking in his wrath as black as
the dæmon whom he served.

The Abbot saw his danger, but faltered not. In the good
old Saxon times, every man was brave, and every brave man
was inured to war, and expert in arms. Calling to his train
to close up, Leofric shouted, "St. Nicholas for Iniscaw!"
and charged home. The fiery onset broke through the
Danish ranks, and left in their gore three of the bravest
there. The way to the Abbey was now open, and all was
clear and safe. But the blood of Leofric was up. He
feared lest the Danes should cut off some of the prickers or
footmen. Wheeling round his horse, and placing himself in
the rear, he covered the retreating force. He shook on high
his boar spear, and remembered the days of his youth, and

seemed more like a gallant Thane, than a cowled monk. Ulf pressed upon him as he backed his steed, and they exchanged thrusts, until blood flowed on both sides, and once the Dane went down. When they had reached the stranger's house, which was just within bowshot of the walls, and the skirmish was well-nigh over, the Abbot halted for a moment, to look back upon his disappointed foe. That moment of delay was, indeed, a fatal one to him. A stray arrow from a Scandinavian bow pierced right through the eye of the Abbot's charger, even unto his brain. It rolled over, stunning its rider in its fall. Before the train, already far in advance, could return to rescue him, Ulf was upon his prostrate foe. He was dragged from the spot, and hurried into the covert, and up the slope. And though the Saxons flung themselves upon their foes, with all the energy of despair, the vantage gained was too great to be repaired. Their zeal and devotion were thrown away. The hunting party had come indeed to a gloomy end. The servant of the cross was vanquished. Leofric the Saxon was a captive in the hands of Ulf the Dane.

"False shaveling!" said the Viking to his prisoner, when they were on board, "False shaveling! I rede ye to know that thou shalt dearly rue the hour in which thou wast bold enough to defy the son of my fathers! I will carve the spread eagle* upon thy vile body, until every bone and muscle

---

* A common torture applied by the Danes to their prisoners was to bind one of them firmly against a tree, with his body naked, and his feet and arms outstretched, and then with a sharp knife to cut the figure of an eagle, with spread wings, upon the breast. By removing the skin, the form of the bird was shown on the raw flesh.

is laid raw and bare, and until thou diest a death viler than that of the unhappy prisoners, whom thou castest down to rot in thy dungeons!"

"False Pagan!" quoth the Abbot, "I would have ye take tent, also, that Leofric the Saxon hath in his veins the blood of a line of kings, yea even of the great Alfred himself. If thou find him mansworn or nithering, like a base serf, bury him in a basket of wickerwork in the next marsh, as was the custom of our forefathers, touching recreants and runagates. Yet it is ill to speak thus. Unworthy servant of the Church though I be, I fear not to look death in the face. And thou, Ulf, art a king's son, therefore it becometh thee not to boast thus largely against a fallen foe."

"By the skull in which my father quaffs mead, and feasts in Valhalla," replied the Dane, "thou speakest sooth, bold monk! The eagle knows the eagle, and the Viking honours the spirit of the brave. To-day shalt thou pledge me in the banquet of bards, and to-morrow thou shalt do me reason."

So they feasted together, the Prince of Denmark, and the Saxon Abbot, in a long and loud carouse. It ended not till midnight. The guests separated, mutually well pleased with each other.

"Pity it were," said Ulf to his armour-bearer, "that this Saxon is a cowled dweller in cloisters. By the shade of Odin, had he been a sea-rover, he would have drained deep draughts from the skulls of his slaughtered foes! I would that he might take service with me!"

Days, however, passed by, and Leofric, though unharmed, was still the guest, rather than the prisoner, of Ulf. In truth, the fault was not with the Abbot. He spoke, often, of his ransom, but could come to no agreement with his captor, whose demands were exorbitant, amounting even to the surrender of the Abbey. So they made no pact, but yet dwelt in fealty together, two bold and fiery spirits, each respecting the other. Sometimes Leofric would speak to Ulf about religion, and endeavour to convert him to Christianity. He would read to him the holy Book, and expound its mysteries, and make them as plain as possible to the somewhat slow and uncultivated mind of the Dane. In some things Ulf was an apt pupil. He loved not the Gospel, and its tidings of peace. But his whole soul kindled, and he brightened with a warrior's pride, when the Abbot read to him of the triumphs of Gideon, and of Joshua, and of the chivalrous Maccabees. Then, indeed, his eye—

"Reddened with its inward lightning,"

and he professed himself enamoured of that glorious faith, and ready to embrace it, and to do battle in its cause. He assured the holy Father that he could now understand why the Saxon brotherhood were such lusty men of war, since they believed in so stirring a creed. The good Abbot felt rather embarrassed at these compliments, and groaned in spirit at the blindness and perverseness of his heathen convert, but he said nothing, being, as it were, in the lion's den, and fearing to arouse the wrath of his martial neophyte.

One day the Abbot had been explaining to him the history of David, whose connection with Jonathan reminded Ulf of their own, and, as old Joinville says, in his quaint French, "son cœur attendrit." But when the Priest spake of the miraculous victory of the shepherd son of Jesse over Goliah, the Dane laughed him to scorn.

" He was but a little man, that same giant Goliah," said
he. " There be in our Sagas many mighty men of renown,
in other days, to whom he would be but a babe. Yea, the
great goddess Fria, herself, is, even according to thy story,
of loftier stature than thy dog of a Philistine. He died the
death he deserved. What bot* were it to be a warrior, and
not be able to defy a boy's sling ? I like not thy champion,
Abbot, nor do I value his arms."

" My son," replied Abbot Leofric, gravely, " do not thou
jest on holy things, which are, peradventure, too hard for
thee."

" Naithless," said Ulf, "though I like well thy God's-spiel,
and specially that portion of it relating to war, wherein did
the Jews approve themselves stout soldiers, I reck little of
thy miracle of a stone. Thine is but a poor hero, gif he
worketh not by manlier weapons, nor in a nobler way.
Such is not the slayer of warriors, such are not the gods of
Valhalla, nor, in our eve of a fight, the " choosers of the
slain."† But come thou, friend Abbot, we will land, and
approach thy walls. It may be that, when they behold thee
in bonds, their hearts will relent, and they will consent to
purchase thy liberty, even at a worthy price."

So they disembarked, and proceeded together to the Abbey.

---

* *i. e.* boot, profit.

† " Such, ere he sheathed his bloody sword,
   As " choosers of the slain " adored
   The yet unchristened Dane.
                              Scott.

   Three weird women were supposed to go through a host, on the eve
of a battle, and select the victims of the morrow.

They approached the building without hesitation, for Leofric was a hostage in their hands, as he walked beside Ulf, and discoursed concerning his ransom. The Abbot's heart was sad and depressed. The words of the proud scoffer had galled him, and had wounded his faith as a Christian man. " Surely," he thought, " this Pagan will not escape scot free. He cometh against us with a sword, and with a shield, and with the weapons of the flesh, but God and St. Nicholas are greater than he ! "

By this time they had reached the walls, upon which were gathered the prior, and the sacristan, and the cellarer, and the obedientiarii, and the cloistered monks and the novices, and the lay brethren, and the men-at-arms ; and great was the outcry, and piercing the wail they made, when they saw their beloved lord a prey to the Egyptian, and a captive to his bow and spear. There was considerable bustle among them, and they conferred together eagerly, and then many of them left the ramparts. Meanwhile Ulf parted a little from Leofric, and advanced towards the Abbey, with the intention of addressing the prior. But he was cut short, and interrupted, in a manner that he little expected. Even as Sisera was smitten by the hand of a woman, and Goliah struck down by the weapon of a peasant boy, so was the great warrior of the Danes, Ulf the red-handed, punished for his blasphemy. One of the cnichts of the Abbey, famed for his skill in the use of the sling, availed himself of a little postern gate, and while Ulf drew near, stole forward and approached him unobserved, under cover of the broken ground. Whirling his little leathern bag round his head, he sent the pebble it contained full at the bosom of Ulf. It entered there, deeply, and mortally. Not a word was spoken, nor did he give a cry, nor did he struggle, but at the feet of the Abbot, and by the very instrument he had reviled, he bowed, he fell, and where he bowed, there he fell dead.

At the same moment a sally was made from the gates, headed by the young cnicht, who had accompanied the Abbot to the chase. The Danes were in no mood to resist. Their hearts melted within them, even as water. They therefore turned and fled. And Leofric was borne in triumph to his old home, with shouts, and congratulations, and smiles, and tears of welcome. The body of the Viking was likewise carried with them, and laid down, in the outer court, beneath the great oak tree in the midst.

There was at first a talk of hanging it on a gibbet, for the crows and kites to tear and rend, but Leofric sternly forbade all such unseemly treatment. Whatever Ulf might have been, bloody, perhaps, and ferocious, yet still he had not used the Abbot unworthily, as, from the bitter feelings existing on either side, he might have been expected to do. So the monk, who, himself a brave man, could appreciate bravery and worth in others, felt respect for his dead foe, and sorrowed over him, as over one that had begun to listen to the truth, and might, perchance, in after days, have been a mighty champion of Christendom. And he looked sadly upon the cold calm features of the royal youth, and bade them prepare him reverently for interment. Ulf could not lie in consecrated ground, for he was unbaptized. A grave was therefore made for him, upon the brow of the pleasant hill that shields the Abbey from the wind. It faced the east, that the sun might, at his uprising, throw a smile upon it.

He was buried, after the fashion of his people, between smooth slabs of stone, and the place of his sepulture was known by tradition as " the Dane's grave."

Long centuries after, one sunny day in spring, a stranger, in whose veins ran the blood of the Danish Vikings, was standing on that very spot. As was before stated, the work-men, plying their pickaxes, broke into an antique grave, lined with large flat stones, and containing the skeleton of a man. There were in it no arms, nor ornaments. But, on a closer examination, there was seen, upon the spot where the breast had been, a round pebble, such as would be fit for a sling. That stone is now on the mantle-piece of the drawing room, at the Abbey. The bones were carefully collected, and buried in holy ground. And we left " the Dane's grave."

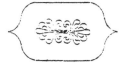

"RATTEZ le Russe," said Napoleon, " et vous trouverez le Tartare." Civilize the Celt, if you please, but his nature constantly betrays itself, as an Australian savage runs away from education, and the restraints of cities, to freedom and his favourite dish of roasted maggots in the wilderness; and as old Blucher replied, when some one told him that Bourmont had become a Royalist, and had mounted a white cockade, " you may stick a peacock's feather in a daw's tail, but the bird is a daw still."

We were at St. Martin's to-day. There, as elsewhere, are the remains of former cultivation, and of a population far more numerous than at the present day. On the island are two small towns. One of them, on the higher ground, facing Crow sound, is neat and comfortable. The valley below it is carefully tilled, and would bear a comparison, both as to husbandry and fertility, with any part of Scilly. The old breed is pretty well extinct here, from frequent crosses. But the lower town has unmistakeable evidence of its Celtic colony, with its dunghills, and pools full of refuse, and general untidiness, and even its poultry, for the Celt loves eggs, and a friend who accompanied me, and who called the place "Pig Town," told me that here was the spot to lay in a stock of them. This was the state of the whole group in Woodley's time. Now the scene is a striking exception to the rest of the property.

A youthful wag, who wanted to describe the grand characteristics of his countrywomen in these islands, once chalked up on the pier at St. Mary's, the following lines:—

> "Scads* and 'taties all the week,
> And a *green veil* on Sundays."

I am sorry to say that not only at St. Martin's, but in other places, this slovenly way of living, and this love of finery, still present a disagreeable contrast.† One reason has been assigned, and perhaps with some truth, for the inferiority of St. Martin's. There is no resident clergyman. The school-

---

* Alas for the truth of this distich ! Scads are no longer caught. The people are too well off to eat them ! Times are changed indeed. Just before the coming of the present Proprietor, salt was six-pence a pound, and the wretched and starving population ate their dried fish without it, not being able to buy. A petition was sent to Government, begging for a remission of the duty, on account of the frightful destitution of the poorer classes, and I believe that some indulgence was shown.

In opposition to this fact I will give an illustration of the state of Tresco now. In the May of this present year there were a few shillings, derived from the offerings at the Sacrament, to be given away, and, out of a population of four hundred and twenty souls, there was some difficulty in finding persons poor enough to be qualified to receive it.

† Parasols are in universal request. In fact I am told that they are even used by girls, when they go milking.

master, who is a dissenter of a sect called the Brianites, now very prevalent here, is the only minister of any denomination in the island. There is at the present day a strong feeling in favour of the Established Church, and of increasing its efficiency. Large sums are lavished upon it, and every attention is paid to its pomp and to its beauty, but when fifty pounds a year would win to Christ such a district as this, there are no funds from which that pittance can be obtained. The Duchy of Cornwall is wealthy, and is hoarding up a large surplus, for what purpose heaven only knows, and it is in vain to ask, and very uncharitable to conjecture. But with all this provident economy on the one hand, and profuseness on the other, this " sui appetens, alieni profusus," it is, it seems, utterly impossible to find sufficient income for a clergyman here, even by uniting the offices of schoolmaster and of curate, as is done at St. Agnes.*

St. Martin's is a singular kind of ridge, rising out of the sea. It appears a long spine, not, I should think, less than two miles and a half long, nor more than three quarters of a mile in breadth. It is principally down, but there are some parts of great richness, and capable of bearing anything, could they only be sheltered from the winds, which blow with a violence irresistible, and hardly to be described. An excellent road is in progress. A few years ago, there was not one wheeled carriage in Scilly. Now there are dozens. And this improvement, with so many others, recently introduced, is to be ascribed solely to the judgment, and

---

* Clerical matters are, indeed, like other things, in rather an exceptional state in Scilly. I was myself lectured by a clergyman on the impropriety of my baptizing *on a Sunday!*

liberality, from which the islands have already so largely benefitted.

The natives are said to be singularly proud of St. Martin's, and to be very jealous of strangers. I could not, for the life of me, help thinking how applicable to this feeling was the beginning of the old monkish canticle "Oh mihi beate Martine," so quaintly parodied by the reformers in the words "All my eye and Betty Martin." By the way, many of our vulgar expressions are derived from this source, that is, from corrupted Latinity, "For the Nonce," "please the pigs" (pyx), "Hocus pocus" (hoc est corpus), are the jests of the day, when a sneer at the ancient faith fell in with the humour of the majority.

The people here are very fond of fine names. Among them are Elmira, Thomasina, Thamasina, Melinda, Emmelina, Florence, Joyce, Honour. And, while on the subject of names, I may add that it is a popular article of belief that a person may be christened a second time. I heard of a girl who disliked her name, which was Joyce, so she re-christened herself Jessie, and Jessie she is called accordingly.

There was not one inhabitant on St. Martin's one hundred and sixty years ago, according to Troutbeck. He described it as unfit for cultivation, while, in another place, he said truly that, in early times, it was tilled universally. I can add to this statement a fact that confirms it strongly. Above the Higher Town there was, many years ago, apparently, a waste of sand. This covering, though about twelve feet deep, was removed by the wind, and below it was discovered good soil, with the ancient enclosures, quite uninjured. A century ago there were but three families here. Mr. Ekins, the first resident steward of the Godolphins, encouraged people to come hither and settle. In Troutbeck's time, the population had increased to thirty families, and one hundred and eighty souls. In Woodley's day there were sixty houses, and about two hundred and eighty people.

At present its inhabitants are not quite so numerous, but its prosperity is very much on the increase. The potatoes grown on it are considered the best in Scilly. Near High Town is the little church, the cemetery of which is the only portion now used.* The church takes here an enforced care for the dead body, while she neglects her duty to the living soul.

A neighbouring eminence, one hundred and sixty feet in height, is crowned with a building called the " Day mark," raised by Mr. Ekins, in 1683, as a guide for ships. Over the door are his initials T. E. with the date of erection.

---

* Since writing the above, I find that an expedient has been adopted, or, rather, has been revived, to remove the evil, though, like most expedients, it only makes matters worse. The curate of St. Mary's goes over to St. Martin's on Sunday afternoon, to do duty there. Now the people are all Brianites, and the schoolmaster, who is a most respectable man, is also, as I have previously stated, the Brianite minister. The islanders have therefore the compulsory service of taking four journeys, backwards and forwards, in all weathers, in order that a clergyman in whom they don't believe, and of whom they know nothing, and see nothing further, may gabble over a few prayers and a sermon, merely to have it said that duty is again done at St. Martin's. These makeshifts do more harm than good. They effect nothing. What is wanted is the presence, the friendly countenance, the example, of a *resident* clergyman. When one of the former chaplains used to go over on Sundays, as is now done, the boatmen often abused him to his face for the trouble he gave them. The church is supported in Scilly from a private source, with the noblest liberality ; and it is a pity that none of its wealthy societies can come forward to its aid.

On a lonely hill,* at the western extremity of St. Martin's, are three objects of greater interest than any other on the island. I allude to the circles, or carns, or barrows, for they partake in part of each character, to be seen there. They are very perfect, though many of the stones have been removed for building purposes. Still, enough remains to show the outline. There, beneath those great rocks, lie the hands that once tilled these lands, and the feet that once trod them. These " warriors of the age of hills " tell us a solemn tale. " How, or when, the nation that dwelt here, became extinct," says Borlase, " we have no means of judging." All we know is that they are gone. Their place knows them not. Like those of Petra, who dwelt in the clefts of the rocks, the men of that forgotten brood lie here, on every headland, each in his stern and lonely sepulchre. The arms that piled above them that mass of stones are dust and ashes like themselves. The Emim, and the Avim, and the Zumzummim of Scripture, are as unreal and as indistinct to our sense as these chieftains. I stand now by the opened cell of one of them, and the words of Ossian come upon me with a strange and appropriate truth :—

" Why dost thou build the hall, son of the winged days ? Yet a little while, and the blast of the desert comes ; it howls through thy deserted courts, and whistles round thy half-worn shield."

The transition from these dim religious dreams to the cultivation and the cleanliness of High Town is certainly unromantic, but it is scarcely unpleasant. The Spaniards have a proverb which is not mal à propos here ; and, indeed,

---

* Called " Cruthers."

it would be difficult to find a circumstance to which they
have not applicable some quaint old saw. That which
occurs to me now seems at first sight rather alien to the
character of that most unpractical and impracticable nation.
They say,—

> " El Primero es el Omnipotente,
>   Y don dinero es su lugarteniente."

> " The chief one is the Omnipotent,
>   And Don Money is his Lieutenant."

I am afraid that even the aspect of this little long rock,
resembling what an Irishman once called " The back bone
of the world, picked by the Ould One," is a proof of the
truth of this saying. The capital spent on these islands by a
generous and skilful hand has developed the resources placed
within their reach by God. We come down from dream-
land, and leave the narrow homes of those to whom worldly
good and evil are now alike of no account, and stand in the
hollow below High Town, and look upon the many traces
of its peace, and plenty. Yet the reputation of the recipients
by no means corresponds with these blessings. The people
of St. Martin's are said to be the hardest and the most
unfeeling of any of the inhabitants of these isles. I have
heard some singular stories of their selfishness and want of
heart, such as the following. The wife of a sick man, who
was very well to do in the world, bought two pounds of
meat for making broth. Before it could be put into the pot
the husband died, and his spouse, seizing the piece of mutton,
ran out of the house, and went round to the neighbours,
trying to dispose of it.

We ascended the steep hill, enjoying at once the prospect,

the walk, and the gleamy sunlight that brightened every object around. My companion was one who had a right to take pride in what we beheld. While we toiled up the ascent, walking slowly, and detained by our remarks on what we saw, I was irresistibly reminded of an anecdote which I once heard adduced, as an evidence of Irish wit and readiness. The Duke of Wellington, as every one knows, is extremely punctual, in keeping even the most trifling appointment. He was one day, when in Ireland, going out —I believe—to dinner, and the horses being such as they usually are in that ingenious country, where you find everything handy but what you really want, came nearly to a stand-still. The Duke put his head out of the window, and swore like forty Pictons, and he, it is said, swore like forty dragoons. At last one of the postillions, a fellow with a rich brogue, and an eye worthy of Lazarillo de Tormes, could stand it no longer. He turned half round on his saddle, and, coolly confronting the angry Duke, addressed him thus:—

" Is it weak you call them, the poor bastes? Sure, its not weak they are at all; your Honour well knows that it isn't the carriage that they feel, *but it's the weight of your Honour's glory that keeps them back!*"

And the rogue beat the Duke, who drew in his head, and held his tongue.

CHAPTER XIV.

A CRUISE ROUND THE WESTERN ISLES.

THE chief boatman and pilot of Tresco is waiting for me, to set off on a sailing excursion to Annet, and the islands of the West.

My conductor is himself a curiosity in his way. He is a handsome, dashing sailor, of first-rate skill in his profession, and as civil and obliging as he is trusty. The people of Scilly speak the purest English of any of the Queen's lieges.* Their correctness both of language and of pronunciation is really marvellous. And our coxswain is quite equal to other Scillonians in this accomplishment. From some circumstance, which it was out of his power to avoid, he was a little behind his time, but it was not his fault that he was so. " I am very sorry to have kept you waiting so long, ma'am," said he, to a lady of our company, " you must have thought me very much wanting in courtesy, in fact, quite a deceiver," and he handed

---

* Some of the phrases used are odd : I asked a man how his wife was, and was told that she was quite "clever and easy,"—that is, well. A person " surprised " is said to be " frightened." " Brave and punctual" signifies " firm." " Rich" means " good."

her over the dank sea weed, and slippery rocks, with a manner
worthy of Sir Charles Grandison.*

We spread our sails to the wind, and ran gaily through
St. Mary's Pool. Here, formerly, lay the frigate of the
Grand Duke Cosmo, receiving and returning the salutes of
the Castle. A little farther on is the rock on which the
Dutch East Indiaman struck and went to pieces, having on
board a treasure of two hundred and fifty thousand guilders,
many of which have been, and are still, picked up. The
lady to whom it belonged was a passenger, and was drowned.
She was proceeding to join her husband, and by this sad
accident, as the account somewhat quaintly adds, " was
prevented from seeing him again." Onward yet a little
more, and we see the scene of the awful disaster that befell
the five families, the whole population of St. Agnes, on their
return from their wedding excursion. Alas for all these
terrible records of wreck and destruction! The sea glances
from our bow in a thousand rainbows, catching the sunlight
on the crest of every wave. A homeward bound corvette

---

* There is a general tone of good breeding in the manners of the
Scillonians that strikes a stranger forcibly. They have a self respect
which gives them confidence, and real dignity, in the presence of their
superiors, and which is very far removed from presumption, or from what
is misnamed independence. When a person addresses you, it is with no
assertion of equality, and yet there is, in the air of people of the lower
orders here, a something indefinable, but striking, and very different from
the subdued demeanour of the English peasantry. If you go into a
cottage, you observe the same thing. The owner, whether man or woman,
does the honours of the house without embarrassment, hands you a
chair with quiet civility, and gives you a simple welcome, with the self
possession of one who knows the place both of the visitor, and of the
host. I certainly never saw in humble life so much good taste, so much
what may be really termed well-bred ease, as at Scilly.

comes within hail, as we go merrily on.   It turns out to be
the old "Lionesse," once the packet to Penzance, but now
altered in her rig, and engaged in the foreign trade.   She
belongs to the port of St. Mary's, and we learn from her
crew, as she passes us, that all is well on board.   Such
incidents are very frequent here, but the voyage home is not
always so lucky.   The wreck of a West Indiaman, the
"Mary Hay," is now in sight, on the shore of Bryher.
And the "Renown," a ship of six hundred tons, from America
to Liverpool, is lying alongside the new pier, waiting to be
broken up.   She took fire, from spontaneous combustion,
beginning, I believe, among some cushew nuts, and her
cargo of cotton and tobacco was almost entirely spoiled.
The hulls of the two wrecks look but sadly amid the gay
rigging and smart finish of the Scillonian vessels, which are
remarkable for their symmetry and neatness.   The glowing
sunbeams seem out of place, upon those battered and dis-
abled veterans.

The swell that sets in between the Garrison and the Gugh
makes our boat, the Crim-scape (so called from being a
waif, saved from a wreck on the Crim rock), dance and heel
over to leeward, till she goes gunwale under, from the
influence of the fresh breeze.   We soon, however, are under
shelter, and abreast of St. Warna's cove.   The grim abode
of the grim Saint, or rather of the sinner, deified by sinners
like herself, frowns down upon us.   We care little for her
malign influence.   Time was that we should have shuddered
to pass her shrine without an offering, or, at least, a depre-
catory prayer.   Now, her memory dwells alone with its
solitude, and her once dreaded name is mentioned only in

connection with a legend or a jest. As for the former of
these two alternatives, she is fortunate in being associated
with it. Considering that these islands are of a respectable
antiquity, and have an historical pedigree of so many centuries, they are sadly unprovided with traditions. There is
not, I believe, a satisfactory ghost in any one of them. And
accordingly a good phantom, a warning spirit, or even a
dream that is verified, are sought in vain. Pixies are among
the things fit to be told to the marines. And lovers of the
supernatural had better buy Mrs. Crowe's book, and find
out an apparition for themselves, for none is seen nor
mentioned here. But all this while we are gliding along
towards Annet, with just motion enough to keep us alive,
as we recline idly in the boat, and listen to the cry of the
puffins from the rocks around.

Annet, or Agnette, little Agnes, has an extent of about
fifty acres. It is entirely uninhabited. Sea birds frequent
it in great numbers, and come here to breed. But it lies
among the breakers treacherously and beautifully still. And
when you look round it, you see desolation almost approaching savage grandeur. We go into our boat and sail on, but
still we find rocks, and still lines of reef, and broken foam,
and little points dotting the surface, and scarcely emerging
from it. We tack and steer in a westerly direction. The
Gilstone that was fatal to Sir Cloudesley Shovel, is pointed
out to us. Everywhere evidences of a land submerged are
spread around us, everywhere danger, everywhere death.
We pass under those fine cliffs that form the western
extremity both of the Gugh, and of Wingletang downs.
The shadows are becoming longer as the day declines, and

lie, ominously dark, upon the bosom of the blue sea. We
talk about the shoals, with which the coast is rife, and tales
of destruction and of wreck are repeated in a sad low tone,
for each speaker is more or less, in his own person, concerned
in some of these. One of them excited a vivid interest, from
the locality in which it occurred, and from the greatness of
the disaster. So I will close my sketch of our little trip by
relating it, as I heard it to-day.

At the beginning of the great French War, and about
the close of the last century, the navy of France was more
powerful, and bolder in its actions, than it became at a later
period, when Nelson had confined the poor remnants left to
it within their ports, and had bequeathed to his successors
the inglorious task of watching and blockading them, as
they rotted away in harbour. When the war first broke
out, expeditions frequently sailed forth, and threatened the
English coasts, and menaced even a descent.

One evening two large vessels were seen, from the heights
of St. Agnes, boldly approaching the island. Their character was unknown. They came on as though they were
friendly, or were sure of the skill of their pilot, making a
glorious show, as the light fell upon their white sails, and
newly painted hulls. They did not communicate with the
shore, nor answer the signals shown. A crowd soon collected, composed of those inured to the sea, whose eyes were
too practised and too keen to be deceived. Their opinion
was formed at once. The strangers were a French ship of
the line and a frigate. They evidently came with hostile
intentions, to make an incursion at least, if not to seize the
islands.

There was no force at hand to repel the attack, if seriously made. All was therefore terror and alarm. A boat was manned and sent across to St. Mary's, to give notice to the garrison of the coming foe. The best and ablest of the males prepared to follow them, hoping to be of some assistance in manning the batteries, and at least to do their duty, if they could effect no more. By the time it was dark, they were gone, and sad and sorrowful were the hearts of those that remained. They could offer no resistance whatever to the landing of an enemy. They could only suffer and be still, should they be doomed to behold, as was most likely, the rifling of their little homes, and perhaps to undergo worse violence at the hands of the ferocious republicans.

In such a manner, and with such anxious forebodings, passed that dreadful night. As soon as morning dawned, those, who had kept their painful watch through the darkness, hastened again to the cliffs. They looked over the broad sea, but they saw nothing. Far away in the distance gleamed a white speck, like a sea-bird's wing. Though already on the horizon, the old sailors pronounced it to be the smaller of the two French vessels. It was evidently alone. Where then was its consort? Where? At some few hundred yards from the western point of St. Agnes was an object that at last caught their attention. Not being able with the naked eye to make it out, they examined it with a glass, and discovered a tricoloured pennant, attached to what was like a flag-staff, and, seemingly, not more than a yard above water. A boat put off to the spot where it lay. When they reached it the mystery was unravelled, the disappearance of the hostile squadron cleared up. The line-of-battle ship had struck upon a sunken rock, and had gone down with all her crew. Her consort had fled in terror. All that was seen of the noble vessel was the pennant that had floated from her mainmast. That slight streamer of silk was the funeral pall of six hundred brave men, who had perished in silence, and in the darkness of the night, their efforts at escape unavailing, their cries for help unheard.

A few bodies only were thrown up by the waves, and were buried in the church-yard of St. Agnes.* The islanders point out their graves, covered simply with turf, for they are strangers who sleep below, and their names none can tell.

---

* Amid the former misdeeds of the islanders, the manner in which the Church was built deserves to be remembered, as a set off. In 1685, a large sum, allotted to them for salvage, was voluntarily devoted, as a free-will offering on their part, to the erection of a house of prayer. Two others had stood, and fallen successively to ruin, near the same spot.

CHAPTER XV.

ST. AGNES.

THE channel between St. Mary's and St. Agnes is seldom still or calm. There is generally a swell rolling in from the ocean, sufficient to tell you that it is a ground upon which you must venture warily, for " that whereon thou standest is hallowed " by many a fearful legend of wreck and disaster. You soon, however, reach the " *Gugh*" a part of St. Agnes once only a peninsula, but, since the time of Borlase, who thus describes it, entirely cut off from the main island at every tide. The Gugh faces the Hugh at St. Mary's. There are many of these Oriental rhymes here, perhaps, derived from the Indo Germanic origin of the Celts, for an Asiatic is so fond of this jingle that, in speaking of Cain and Abel, he alters the former to *Kabel*, to

make it correspond with Abel.   You land upon the neck of
sand, at a place called Perconger, or Porth-conger, bay.   It
is a curious fact that at both extremities of the islands you
arrive at a spot so named.   The rock of Scilly outside
Bryher is supposed to be termed thus from Silya, which, as
I mentioned before, is the Cornish for conger.   Climb the
hill above your landing-place.   If you have in your nature
a spark of romance, or the slightest sense of natural beauty,
if you can feel the sublime language of that solitude, where
the spirit communes with God, and God with it, stay and
enjoy an hour spent, perhaps, as you never spent one before.
Should you be like the son of a Highland Chieftain, who,
on my asking him if he liked the poetry of Burns, replied
contemptuously " No, he is so vulgar ; " or should your taste
be that of the young French lady, who, at her first sight of
the Alps, exclaimed "Ah que c'est gentil ; " go back to your
boat, and dismiss the Gugh from your mind for ever.   The
case is not an improbable one.   Enthusiasm is sometimes
qualified as that " which makes us mad."   My poor friend
Haydon was considered insane for reciting Shakspeare aloud.
Some early acquaintances of mine once called upon me,
after a lapse of many years.   I had filled my house with
antique furniture, old Indian china, and plate, and was, in
Lord Byron's words, " guilty of being innocent" of the fact
that my hobby was somewhat singular, and that few would
sympathise with it.   We had been looking at a magnificent
carved oak bed, which, with its crimson curtains, and suite
of massive fittings, was, in my eyes, the perfection of solemn
and ancient splendour, when one of my guests suddenly
cried out, " Good heavens, where did you pick up all this

hideous rubbish?" There is in the world a multitude, perhaps a great majority, of persons who feel thus. They are all the happier for it. Those keen, and fine, and exquisite sensibilities, that charm and win us, bring no blessing to their possessors. So if you are, fortunately for yourself, insensible to the stern beauty of that haunted down, with its carns, its rifled sepulchres, and all its wild ancestral memories, go home, and thank God for it.

Over the whole extent of the Gugh are scattered rocks of every shape, many of them being more pointed than I have seen in the other islands. There are likewise a number of circles, some of which are small, and others of the usual extent, containing those large sepulchres, which, from their size, seem to have belonged to a family rather than to an individual. There is also a menhir,* as it is called in Brittany, or tall upright rock for worship. From the quantity of little funeral rings still remaining, one would suppose this spot to have been a general burying place. The names of some of the points are very quaint, for there is Wetnose and Dropnose! These fanciful appellations are to be found everywhere in the footsteps of the Anglo Saxon race. In the midst of the sounding terms furnished by Oriental hyperbole, you come upon them strewn here and there. As you sail out of the Indus, you round a bold headland. Nearchus gave it a fine Greek designation, but the English christened it Cat's-head, and Cat's-head it remains.

---

* I suppose this is the derivation of the Cornish name Tremenheere—Tre-menhir.

From the extremity of the Gugh you see a rock which has retained a melancholy interest. It is the Gilstone. In October 1707, as I stated in my account of Porth Hellick bay, the Association,* the flag-ship of Sir Cloudesley Shovel, with two other ships of the line, the Eagle and the Romney, struck here and were lost, with two thousand men. In fact, standing upon this headland, and looking over the innumerable peaks and shoals, extending for miles in every direction, one ceases to wonder at the Scillonian proverb, "that for one man who dies a natural death, nine are drowned;" or at the complaint of Mr. Tucker, in his report to the Prince of Wales, that the chief hindrance to making a roadstead, and harbour of refuge, arose from the prejudice of sailors against it. The Colossus, of the line, was lost here, with, I believe, all her crew; so was the Nubicto; so were the Thames steamer, and the Douro; nor is this all. Many a wreck takes place, and the deep swallows up all memory of the disaster. In 1842, the top-mast of a vessel was observed above water, not far from the shore of St. Agnes. She proved to be the " William Proben " from Shields, but there ended all knowledge of her. Her sailors were drowned. She lay there, as men saw her, but they were ignorant of all else connected with her. The disappearance of vessels is so common as to excite little surprise. The woman who waits upon me has been married two years. Her husband, who was mate in an outward bound trader, when he was last heard of, sailed from some foreign port four months since, but no further tidings

---

* It is sometimes called the " Victory."

have reached her, and she has gone into service without
a murmur. Setting aside " the dim twilight of the laurel
grove" that clothes the Isles of Greece, these rocks resemble
them as they are described by Byron :—

> " Fair clime, where every season smiles
> Benignant o'er those " Blessed Isles,"
> *　　*　　*　　*
>
> " Where mildly dimpling, *ocean's cheek*
> *Reflects the tints of many a peak,*
> Caught by the laughing tides, that lave
> Those Edens of the Eastern wave."

In both cases, the beauty is rendered mysterious and solemn
by its associations, at least to those who think and feel.
Those who do not are little worth. " I do not envy the
man," says old Samuel Johnson, very truly, " whose bosom
does not beat with patriotism on the field of Marathon, or
with piety amid the ruins of Iona."

Cross the neck of sand at Perconger, and ascend a little
slope. You will then find yourself in the main town of St.
Agnes, which boasts a population of about two hundred,
nearly every other man being named Hicks. Here is the
pretty Parsonage, and the school. The clergyman fills both
offices, being both curate and schoolmaster, an arrangement
much wanted at St. Martin's. A little farther on is the
lighthouse with its revolving beacon.* These are in excellent order. But oh ! ye rulers of the Trinity-house, men of
good intentions ye may be, and of high nautical science, but
alas for your taste ! The residence attached to the establish-

---

* It is well worth a visit. There are three faces, and ten lights in
each face, which is visible for a minute, the entire revolution being
effected in three. The large reflectors are of silver, and have been in
use for nearly fifty years, but are still as bright and fresh as ever.

ment is large, larger in fact than is requisite. It is built very expensively. The doorposts are of granite ; the chimneys, elegantly carved, are of Portland stone ; and the Palladio or Wren of the Trinity House has most carefully *painted them!* Below the lighthouse is the small church, and a beautiful little model farm-house, built of course by the Proprietor, to whom is due the credit of every improvement, and from whom every plan, for the comfort and benefit of the islanders, meets with a generous and disinterested support.* The bay beneath is a curious specimen of etymological corruption. It is called Prigless,† or Priglis, the proper phrase being Portus Ecclesiæ, or Church bay. There is here another word, the root of which I cannot unravel. It is " Sant-aspery-neck." Probably, as Mazeppa says, it is " some lurking saint," but who he may be passes man's powers to discover.

Above the town is a wide down called Wingletang, which, like the Gugh, almost approaches sublimity. It presents a marvellous contrast to the cultivated fields behind, and to the soft blue sea, and to that azure haze above your head. You find, as soon as you reach it, a very remarkable rock called " the Devil's Punch-bowl," with a large basin on the top. Borlase says that it is a Logan, and may be moved by pushing it with poles. It is, at all events, a very grand and striking object. Indeed over the whole extent of

---

* A pedlar, with whom I was talking one day, said to me that seventeen years ago all the people here were paupers, but now "they are all gentlemen."

† Priglitz, however, is pure Saxon, and is now the name of a Saxon village.

Wingletang down, and on the Gugh, are scattered profusely the finest and most picturesque masses of stone, no two alike, but bearing this resemblance (as has been observed), that they all dip to the north. You have here an excellent view of the western isles, and, amongst others, of Annet; but your heart sickens as you look upon their fantastic outlines, and pinnacles just emerging from the water, studding it with so many deaths. Having made the circuit of the moor, we arrived at a little cove, or bay, lying between immense masses of rock, as calm, and happy, as

> " Vallombrosa, where the Etrurian shades
> High overarched embower."

The circle here was no woven fretwork of leaves, but a great wall of granite, frowning above the turf at its foot. It is the very scene for a marvel, for its aspect prepares the mind for one. And a marvel is ready to your hand. This island was formerly dedicated to *St. Warna*,* an Irish saint, who landed here one day in a coracle, or boat of wickerwork covered with skins, from the green isle. Her maidenhood must have been a sad loss to the bachelors of those days. What a sailor's wife the lady would have made, and how she would have spliced the main brace! Be that as it may, the good islanders, very naturally, believed that so bold a voyager must be a patroness of those who live by the sea, in more senses than one, for her holiness was supposed to preside, not only over fair sailing, but over foul, since her

---

* Pronounced Santa Waund. Does this give a clue to the unknown root of the word Santaspery—Santa-pery, or Bury? There are several names resembling this, in Cornwall and Devon—Perran, Buryan, Berry; and all derived from Ireland.

power extended to wrecks. Her shrine was here, and here is even now the site of her mystical well,* into which whoever drops a pin (as into that of St. Winifred), and utters a wish, will obtain what they seek. People pray generally according to their tastes. The Scillonians usually asked for wrecks; and I have heard of one man, who threw a pin into the little basin, with these words "at least a first rate Indiaman."

In former days St. Warna played a very conspicuous part in all transactions hereabouts. The Reformation by no means put an end to her empire. The fiery race of "Hicks,"† whose squabbles with that of "Mortimer" show that the ladies of that house were well skilled in the language peculiar to the apostolic occupation of the sale of fish, practised by their lords, seems to have warmly patronized the Irish saint. As Cadmus, when he emigrated with Moses, in the Exode from Egypt, introduced the use of letters into Greece, so St. Warna appears to have introduced the culture of the shillelah,‡ which has since flourished here,

---

* It is nearly filled up.

† The old Court books, which I was permitted to inspect through the kindness of Mr. Augustus Smith, are infinitely amusing as to the habits of these insular belligerents. In one case, "Hicks versus Mortimer," for scandal, in which the plaintiff accused the defendant of having had a child more than the law allowed, and the defendant rejoined that "if she had, she had at least not killed it," the Bench most impartially imposed a good fine upon *both* parties, and made them share the burden of the costs. The ducking-stool, for scolds, formerly a frequent mode of punishment, must have been very often set to work. Nor were the magnates of justice very particular as to the sex of these recipients of their judicial bounties. One woman, for theft, received, at the public whipping-post, forty stripes!

‡ Another Irish peculiarity, possessed by these islands, is that no snake, nor any noxious reptile, is to be found here.

as never did thorn at Glastonbury. In fact her clients, the Hicks, are a true Celtic race, masculine, untidy, touchy, litigious, given to fun, strong liquors, and scandal, wielding a hoe for potatoes with one hand, and brandishing a blackthorn with the other.

I learned many of these historical anecdotes by the side of the ancient basin, now well nigh choked up. The age of unbelief has succeeded to the age of miracles. The islanders, literally, don't care a pin for St. Warna. An old man discoursed with me of the past, as we stood on the site of her vanished shrine, and the scene of other days arose vividly before my mind's eye. I could see the country folk coming to kneel before the rude figure of their Idol, and to pray for wrecks. So the Roman peasant brings her child to bow in prayer before the image of the Madonna, and to lisp its orisons to " Mamma," as has been done so often in my hearing. The amphitheatre of rock looked down upon them, as it now frowned upon us. The great sepulchres on yonder hill were then as yet unviolated, and the sleep of the buried warriors undisturbed. The population was numerous and wealthy, before war, and natural convulsion, and the elements, had played their part in disuniting and depopulating these " Islands of the Blest."*

> " How soon that day of splendour was o'ercast,
> That bright brief day, too beautiful to last."

By degrees the dwellers in the land dwindled away, until even the pathetic language of Scripture was inapplicable to their lot, for there was not a single inhabitant abiding here, who could say " and I, even I only, am left to tell the tale."

---

* Scilly was supposed to be the " Fortunata insulæ " of the ancients.

" How was this brought about ?" quoth I to the patriarch, who babbled to me of these by-gone events.   His reply was, in substance, as follows, and we will call his tale—

THE LEGEND OF ST. WARNA.

THE LEGEND OF ST. WARNA.

ONCE upon a time, very long ago, when from frequent inroads, and civil broils, the whole country was brought down into a low and feeble state ; when law was so little known, or so little regarded, that a man who did wrong was, at the mere will of his lord,* placed on a rock with some bread and water, and left to be washed off, and drowned, by the receding tide ; when the good old days of Earl Richard, and Earl Edmund, and Earl Reginald, were remembered with regret; there dwelt in St. Agnes five families only, and those of the poorest class. The old faith had been supplanted by one plain and stern, the tabernacles of our Fathers had everywhere been thrown down, and ruined, and the sons and daughters of prayer were driven forth, from their peaceful cloisters, into a strange and unknown world. Many there were, in those times, who disdained to purchase life by submission. Many there were who refused to partake of the new rites, or to enter their churches, and who said in the spirit, peradventure in the

* See Appendix.

AA

very words, of the Hebrew Prince, when threatened with danger at the hands of an apostate from their erst common belief, " Shall such a man as I go up into the Temple to save my life ? I will not go up !"

But others from coarser and darker motives clave to their antique worship. The power, that dwelt in St. Warna, was believed to be strong over those who followed their business on deep waters. Many a time, when a gallant ship was seen approaching land, in fancied safety, walking grandly upon her way, the dim shadow of the hostile Saint was thought to appear, brooding, like a cloud, above her, and leading her, unconsciously, upon some one of the concealed terrors that lurked below. Many a time a light burning upon the shore, like a friendly signal, hurried the homeward bound bark, and her trusting company, upon rocks from which no human hand could rescue them. In all these cases, St. Warna was held to be the presiding influence, the unseen shade, that did her terrible spiritings even at her own stern will. So, when the holy rood was pulled down, and the shrines defaced, and their relics scattered abroad, and people went about breaking down the carved work thereof, and shivering into fragments the images, and crying out, " these be thy Gods, oh Israel !" the few remaining inhabitants, yet abiding on St. Agnes, clung to their old faith more fervently, perhaps because it was fallen ; perhaps also because they feared lest the new one should, by depriving St. Warna of her supposed authority over the elements, rob them of the profits derived from the frequent wrecks, which they believed her to have driven upon their rugged shores.

At that period, as I before said, five families alone

were left upon St. Agnes. They were unwilling to admit
strangers among them, lest they should be obliged to share
the advantages of their wicked gain with a greater number,
and so diminish their unholy store. They bowed daily
before the altar of St. Warna, and daily threw pins into her
well, and offered up their supplications for wrecks. Many
of these there were, and their hearts were gladdened, and
they grew wealthy on their spoils. The corpses of the
crews they stripped, and then flung them back into the sea.
Some missionaries of the reformed belief essayed to come,
and teach them the things that concerned their peace, but the
islanders stoned them, and drove them away. Even as the
Idolaters of Ephesus cried "Great is Diana of the Ephesians,"
so did they magnify St. Warna, the source of their bad
prosperity. They were like the leeches, ever craving for
more blood, for they were still unsatisfied, even by the
abundance of their ill-got goods.

People prophesied against them, and foretold for them an
evil end, but those of St. Agnes were ever, and are now, a
dour race, disagreeing among themselves, and only uniting
to oppose some common enemy. So they went on sacrificing
to St. Warna, and laying snares for unhappy mariners,
and increasing their profits, at the expense of their souls.
The preachers of the Gospel faith held that the Demon was
permitted, for a time, to personate the Saint, and so to do these
works of darkness; and truly it seemed probable, for they
prospered in their ungodliness, and even went so far as to
take up their parable against the new ministers, and stoutly
appealed to their well-doing, as a proof of the efficacy of
their prayers, and of the influence of St. Warna.

One day a vessel was seen to approach the island, in a quarter the most dangerous and, generally, the most carefully avoided. All the five households of St. Agnes were on the alert. They knelt before the shrine, and vowed their offerings, in case their prayers were heard. They then hurried to the shore, and saw there, as they believed, a plain proof of the power of their patroness.

The vessel had, by some almost miraculous chance, passed Annet, with its wide reefs and shoals. Tempted by the appearance of deep water and safe anchoring ground, the crew bore up and made straight for the shore. For some time there was no sign of danger. The tall ship came on bravely, and without fear. At last, however, the foam ahead gave notice of breakers on the bow, and the helmsman endeavoured to wear, but in vain. The devoted craft missed stays, and was next moment lifted upon a sharp rock, the peaks of which pierced her sides, and held her fast. She struggled and reeled to and fro, but every shock lengthened her agony, and the water rushed in through the leak thus made, and then, as her stout timbers gaped and yawned from each successive blow, she parted amidships, and the sea was covered with her fragments. Her crew and passengers were beheld in the water, swimming with the energy of despair, or clinging to portions of the wreck, on which they hoped to reach the shore. But man held out to them no helping hand. One by one, they sunk, and were seen no more. The wretched islanders watched their expiring struggles, but made no effort to aid them. All their exertions were directed towards seizing and dragging forth, high and dry, upon the beach, such articles of value as the tide had already begun to cast up. While they were thus engaged, a mass of timbers was borne to the strand, unnoticed by those around. Three or four times it was left, apparently, by the waves, and was again as often sucked back amid the breakers. Yet, loud as was the howling of the wind, and the thunders of the angry deep, there issued from among them a cry awfully distinct and clear. It caught the ears of some of those rude pillagers, and made them for a moment pause. It came from that heaving fragment of woodwork, which had so nearly been flung clear upon the land, but to which the billows clung with such desperate and fierce tenacity.

As it whirled round in the vortex formed by the advancing and retiring currents, there were seen upon it two objects that well might excite compassion, and stir up to the rescue even those little accustomed to pity, or to spare. A white-haired and reverend man, in the dress of a Priest of the reformed faith, was lashed firmly to a plank, and held in his arms a beautiful child. It was the plaintive appeal of the latter that had penetrated through the roaring of the storm. The patriarch uttered no cry, made no complaint, but, still holding the infant clasped to his bosom, looked piteously to those on shore. It was a sight to touch the heart of a savage, but it made no impression upon the wreckers. They gazed coolly and callously upon that struggle between man and the elements. They felt a kind of curiosity as to the result of the strife. But they had no pity, and they never moved a step nor a hand to aid.

The contest was a short one. Every wave, as it broke over the frail raft, weakened the vital powers of the old minister, already enfeebled by the previous trials, and horrors, of the day. His eye lost its expression, a quick shiver from time to time passed over his limbs, his face assumed a livid paleness, and he became by degrees insensible to his sufferings, and his perils. Still, however, the instinct of love was strong within him. He never for a moment relaxed his clasp of the child. He seemed, in his agony, and at the moment of dissolution, to cling closer to that tie, whatever it might be, which even now was next his heart. As he grew feebler, so did the little object of his care and love wax fainter too. The cry sunk into a wail, and the wail into a stifled moan, and then nothing was heard but a sharp convulsive sob, and then again all was still. Close strained in each other's arms the aged and the infant dead lay there, happily beyond the consciousness of sorrow, or of pain. The raft rolled round and round in the furious eddies, but the plashing of the waters upon it was the only reply it gave. The Divine had ceased to inhabit the earthy, and had gone, no one knew whither, to tell its tale of wrong, and to ask for redress from God.

That night the grim leader of the wreckers was lying in bed, when he saw a vision. It might have been a dream, a vivid and lifelike dream, or it might have been a fearful reality; for if ever ghosts, in the words of Ossian, " ride upon the storm," it must be after such dark and unhallowed deeds.

There stood, or there seemed to stand, beside his bed, two figures. One of them was the old man who was drowned in the catastrophe of that morning. He was pale, as he had seemed in life, but the expression of his countenance was changed. It had undergone such a transfiguration as death only effects, when the mortal puts on immortality, and assumes the dignity of an undying spirit. His eye was no longer pleading with sad eloquence, in the name of God, and of humanity, for a mercy which was denied. His brow was solemn and majestic, rather than stern. It had passed through the ordeal of the grave, and had borrowed from its depths a power which life cannot possess. The other figure was one with which the islander was well acquainted. It was the Saint, before whose rudely sculptured form he had so often knelt, and prayed. It was, in a mockery of existence, the similitude of her graven image in stone. It was St. Warna.

The child of the new faith, and the canonized representative of the old worship, stood face to face, silently regarding each other. Then the ancient woman, raising her arm, by an impulse that was not like an act of life, stretched it over the pallet, on which lay the trembling wrecker, and said, in accents low and clear,—

" Apostle of strange doctrines, why comest thou hither to trouble us before our time? These are my children, therefore do thou harm them not."

The lips of the old man moved not, yet he spake.

" Teacher of deceits," said he, " and of a faith of dæmons, thou and thy children shall soon be no more. Their hour, and thine, is come. They that live by wrecks, shall perish by a wreck. The moon shall not reach her full, ere this isle of sin, and murder, shall be desolate; they who pollute it now shall die the death they have given to others; thy shrine shall be left worshipless, and be cast down, and disappear from the face of the earth, even as a tale that is told. This is the Lord's doing, and it is marvellous in our eyes! "

The voice ceased; there was silence; the two ghostly phantoms lingered for a moment, and then melted into thin air. The terrified man strained his eyeballs, and gazed into space, but he saw nothing. He listened, but all was still.

The impression made by this ghostly interview did not outlive the hours of darkness. Next day the hardened sinner went about his plunder as usual. He spoke to others of the occurrences, but they laughed at his relation. The young girl, to whom he was affianced, jested with her lover about his lonely situation, that made him suffer from ill dreams. So he held his peace, and turned his attention to gathering his share of the wreck, and to preparing for his wedding, which was to take place in a day or two at Ennour,* or, as it is now called, St. Mary's.

The morning, fixed upon for its celebration, arrived. It was dark and lowering. The channel between the Gugh and the bay of Old Town, always disturbed, was now agitated with a heavy swell from the eastward, while the wind, as is usual from that quarter, was puffy, and blew in squalls. Naithless the whole of the five families embarked in their boats, and after a stormy passage, reached Tolman head in safety. Sorely and unwillingly had the inhabitants of St. Agnes consented to enter a church of the reformed creed, and to have a marriage celebrated among them according to its rites. The good Clerk rebuked them for their idolatrous practices, and they retaliated on him with bitter and profane scoffs. And when they left the church, the last words that passed between them were of warning on the one side, and of scorn and defiance on the other. So, and in such a spirit,

---

* Ynys-more, great island.

the people of St. Agnes set out upon their return home.
They left that shore, but they never reached their own alive.
The wind had increased to a gale, and from a gale to a
tempest. Scarcely had they got beyond the Pulpit rock,
and on a level with that which is called " the Gull," when a
tremendous sea broke over them, and hurried, at once, to the
bottom, the whole of their little fleet. Of the crews, not one
person escaped, neither was one of the bodies recovered.
The boats, as if conducted by an avenging Providence,
drifted across the strait, and were found, some time after,
deposited by the tide in St. Warna's bay. In this sort the
prediction of the ship-wrecked Divine was accomplished.
No human being remained on St. Agnes; nor was it again
peopled for many a day ; nor was the worship of St. Warna
ever renewed. Her shrine escaped the violence of the
Iconoclasts, owing to its situation, for none visited nor saw
it; but it could not avoid the inroads of Time, which, in the
words of Bacon, " innovateth greatly indeed, but gently,
and by degrees scarcely to be perceived." With the lapse
of years, the progress of decay became more rapid. Settlers
again sought the island, and as they were men, who knew
not St. Warna, they did not reverence her little retreat. So
it gradually mouldered away. Her well was filled up by
neglect rather than by any act of violence, and her name
lived only in some legend or tradition, connected with the
wild times, and the wild dwellers, of the past. In the train
of the reformed faith, came in gentler and purer doctrines,
bringing glad tidings of good things. The smuggler forgot
his craft; the wrecker ceased to ply his terrible trade; the
beauty of holiness was taught by a ministry derived from

those Fathers of the Gospel Faith, one of whom died upon
that beach, in the days when men bowed down before stocks
and stones.   So while we regret much that the past has
taken from us, let us prize that which the present still enjoys.

When we quit the hill-side, the evening sun plays around
the grey rocks, and green slope, of St. Warna's bay.   As it
goes down, we are left in shadow, but its beams still linger
round the little church above.   There is a beautiful and an
affecting moral in what is thus passing before our eyes.
The Faith of other days lies in shadow, desolate and
forgotten, while the Faith in which we walk to-day basks
in the light which is from God.   The brightness of Scripture
truth hath wrapped it in a glory, unshared by its deserted
rival below.   When all else is dark, the departing gleams
from Heaven have rested on it for a while ; " the dayspring
from on high hath visited " it.

CHAPTER XVI.

POPULAR SUPERSTITIONS.

THESE are not rife in Scilly. There is in the islands as little of romance, and as much of matter of fact, and of common-place, as would be looked for in a Manchester mill. In fact, the sentimental is discouraged, and the practical set up in its place, until the lovers of the marvellous find themselves quite out of their element, and very much in the position of a friend of mine, who had lost his head groom, a clever, but wicked fellow, and who remarked to a hanger-on in the stables, "that Tom had gone to the Devil at last." "Lord, sir!" replied the worthy supernumerary, "does a great gentleman like you believe in the Devil?"

I have before remarked that the absence of ghostly legends is a strong proof of a change of race, in these islands. It has always been so. The Longobard, or Aleman, never troubled himself with the apparitions of his Roman predecessors. The Arab knew nothing of Gothic marvels, beyond the story of Count Julian and la Cava. The Norman warrior sneered at, and buried in oblivion, the

Saxon hobgoblins of Croyland or of Ely. All the tales of
Irish spectres belong to the Fanshawes and the Beresfords,
to the Lords of the pale. And thus it is with Scilly. The
whole population dates no further back than from the days
of Cromwell. It is entirely modern, having its tales of
horror indeed, but relating only to smuggling, and wrecking,
and disasters akin to them. The most remote of these dark
scenes scarcely remounts up to a period of a hundred years
ago. The shades of the departed race that peopled these
rocks, when they formed a wide and smiling land, may
hover around the heaths on which we still see their tombs,
and circles, and altars, but the eye of modern unbelief
beholds them not, the voice of no descendant records their
exploits, the song that celebrated them, and the hearts in
which that song found an echo, are alike cold and still.

The only part of the islands in which I have met with
any spectral records of respectable antiquity, is Tresco. I
stumbled there by mere chance upon a trace of some ghosts,
with a pretence to a decent ancestry. They would be held
in little respect by such persons as the worthy Gael, who,
on hearing the name of a countryman mentioned, replied
contemptuously, " Pooh, the upstart only came in with
Fingal." In fact, the oldest of my spirits is supported by
the high authority of the great grandfather of my informant;
so, after all, the *revenant* is only a visitor of yesterday, and
may be well ashamed of his shadowy pedigree.

Where Tresco Abbey now stands, there stood formerly
a religious establishment. This was plundered at the
Reformation, and had the finishing touch put to its tale of
ruin at the Great Rebellion. On its site, and resting against

the walls of the old Church, four or five cottages gradually arose, built of the consecrated materials, intruders upon hallowed ground, and forming, by the scenes perpetrated in them, and by the characters of their occupants, a fearful contrast to the memory of what had once existed there. The principal inhabitants of these cabins all belonged to a family now, I believe, extinct, but, in those days, rather numerous. One of them was, in two ways, distinguished from his neighbours. He was pre-eminent for wickedness— even in those times of piracy and plunder—and for his faculty of seeing supernatural appearances. He was even visited, as my informant worded it, by the " evil one" himself, for I observe that a true Scillonian—like a real Celt—never mentions Satan by name, just as an Irishman speaks of " the good people," that is, the fairies.

Now Dick the wicked, who dwelt in the desolation of the sacred precincts, feared neither their associations, nor the remembrance of the deeds of strife and violence since committed there. He was a man, it was said, who defied all agencies, human, diabolical, and divine. His life had been spent in the midst of lawless deeds, and he had grown old and infirm in the quiet nook, whose blessed influences had never moved his spirit to aught but a revolting jest. It was his boast that he had been often met, face to face, by those who were not of earth. Near the spot where the present farm buildings stand, some tale was told of a poor shipwrecked Dutchman, who was murdered and buried * in

---

* The islanders refused burial in consecrated ground to those cast ashore from wrecks. The bodies of all who died in this manner were interred in the sand, or on the downs. Many little carns, or heaps of stones, mark the sites of these hasty graves.

the sandbank. People feared to visit the spot after night-
fall. But the old wrecker had no such scruples. Often, he
said, when he passed, the form of the dead man was seen
pacing gloomily up and down, by the side of the present
road. He never spoke, nor, when spoken to, did he reply,
but moved silently onward, and, at the end of his beat,
turned back again. The path to the ruins then mounted
over the Abbey hill. The old sailor was once going along
it, when he suddenly encountered the apparition of a deceased
person, whom he had known. There is an idea prevalent
that a ghost, on meeting any one, always takes the right
hand. It did so on this occasion. The fiery blood of Dick
the wicked was up in a moment. " What!" said he, " dost
thou take the right hand of me!" The shade answered
not, but turned and followed him to his door, and there only
left him. On another occasion, he was passing through
the burial ground, and entering his house, and there he
remembered him of an ancient comrade in his wildest scenes,
who had now gone to his account, and was sleeping quietly
in the turf beneath his feet. It appears that they had often,
in former days, spoken of one of them, in case of death,
visiting the survivor. As yet the promise, made by him that
was departed, was unfulfilled. Dick was pondering on
these old passages of his early life, and, as he crossed his
threshold, he called out " Johnny, Johnny, wilt thou not
keep thy word?" Even as he spoke, there was a report like
thunder, so terrible, that his hat, as it were, rose upon his
bristling hair, while it stiffened with intense horror, and, in
that fearful sound, his friend's voice seemed to reply. It
appeared to shake the walls and the roof, until they trembled

again. Many times he heard calls in the night, and an invisible hand moved his clothes and his squalid furniture about.

At last, after innumerable glimpses of spiritual life, and communings with the dwellers in another world, Dick, one night, received a still darker summons. He had been long bedridden, but was neither cured of his evil passions, nor converted from his evil ways. One midnight, some visitant, at whom it was impossible to do more than guess, entered his room. Next morning he was found, wrapped in a long loose coat which he was in the habit of wearing, at a considerable distance from his house. It was whispered that One, scarcely more wicked than himself, had thus essayed to bear him bodily away. He died soon after, believing that Satan had been the agent in this mysterious flitting, but fearless and hardened to the last.

His son was the last of the family who possessed this sort of second sight. He was rather an improvement on his father, but still he was evidently " no great shakes." One evening, he brought his horse down to an outbuilding in the churchyard, and was engaged in foddering it, when he felt the animal start and tremble violently. He looked up, and saw, standing on the hedge (that is, the wall), the figure of a man, pale, grim, and stern, clad in an antique garb, and wearing on its head a three-cornered hat. He turned away in terror, and leaving the animal tethered, as he thought, securely, walked to his own abode. But the presence of the Unearthly was too much for the poor beast. By a strong and sudden effort, it broke the halter, and was at its master's door as soon as he.

Some years ago, when the cabins yet stood about the haunted churchyard, and the whole place possessed that evil reputation which it has scarcely lost, some young men were strolling among the tombs, and jesting lightly, and in a scoffing manner, respecting the terrors of other times. One of them, bolder or more careless than the rest, uttered a sort of invocation, or defiance, against the shadows, that were supposed to claim the consecrated precincts for their inheritance. He had just uttered the words of the psalm,—

> "As wind blows chaff away,
> So, in the presence of the Lord,
> The wicked shall decay."

when a sudden burst, as of thunder, was heard above and around, enveloping, as it appeared, the scorner himself, and lifting from his head his hat, which was whirled round and dashed against the wall. The electric shock, or whatever it might be, made a great impression on the thoughtless party, and sent them away frightened indeed, if not cured.

The old man who died lately, aged ninety-six, at Bryher, was said to see visions. His wife, who had departed this life long years ago, came to his bed, as he believed, every night, with many an appearance of glory, and angelic shapes, and spirits from another world. The patriarch was evidently held in respect, among his children and his children's children. The shadows, and the mysteries of an age gone by, seemed to invest him with a peculiar sanctity, and to give him the ghostly privileges, which are denied to the stern and practical habits of to-day.

Witches are a Scillonian article of faith. Formerly they were said to swarm at Tresco. The son of Dick the wicked got a taste of their quality that he found somewhat unpalatable. Walking, one evening, near the present farm buildings, he beheld five old women, of the true sort for Hopkins the witch-finder, executing, by moonlight, a kind of dæmon dance, and riding, as it were, on sticks that were placed, after the fashion of children's hobby-horses, between their legs. He came upon their ghastly merriment unawares. All at once the sport stopped. One of them, a virago of his own blood, called to him by name, and bade him go home, and see that he spoke to none of what he had beheld. But the poor man in his horror almost lost his senses, and either forgot, or disregarded the injunction, for he related the occurrence to his wife. In case of disobedience, he had been threatened with a mark of their wrath, which he should bear to his grave. He had long black hair. When he got up next morning, it was as white as snow!

Again, one of the same brood came down, one day, to a neighbour's house, and tried to sell him a sheep and lamb, but the price asked was so exorbitant, that the farmer refused to deal. The old woman departed, muttering strangely. That evening a choice ram, belonging to the poor man, died. Another of the flock followed daily, till ruin stared him in the face. At last, he went off to consult a weird sister on the course he should pursue. She advised him to kindle a huge fire, and to burn the next animal that died. The holocaust was soon ready, for on going to the field he found an ewe cold and stiff. He lighted a large pile of furze, and placed the sheep upon it. As the flames blazed up, he raised his eyes, and saw, close to him upon the hedge, wrapped in her little red cloak, and grinning diabolically, the hag, the cause of all this mischief, though she was then, bodily, in her own house! And from that time, the plague was stayed.

In the old days of wrecking, and of worse deeds, many crimes were committed that might well be supposed to bring back the victim to the scene of his sufferings and his wrongs. About sixty years ago, a large merchantman was captured by a pirate, and afterwards retaken, and brought into Scilly. She lay alongside the old pier. One, who was then a youth, and whose daughter told me the story, went on board. She had no middle deck. As he was looking through the cracks in the partition, where it would have been, had there been one, he saw what seemed a kind of hen-coop, newly painted green, and against it was the figure of a gentleman dressed in a dark suit with high boots, and falling lace collar, and a three-cornered cocked hat on his head. The lad looked long and earnestly, to make sure of the fact. He then mentioned it, and inquiry was made, but nothing could be seen or heard of the shadowy visitant. There was no speech nor language that told its tale.

Some years afterwards, the youth had become a man, and was in the service of the state. Another vessel was brought into port, under suspicious circumstances, and he, with a brother officer, was placed in charge of her. It was his watch, and he sate, one evening, in the state cabin, as he thought, alone. Opposite to him was a large arm chair, apparently empty. As he gazed on it mechanically, he saw in it the figure of a gentleman richly habited, holding in his hand an instrument of music, and on his knee sate a little boy, who was playing with him, and clasping his neck. As he stared upon the apparition, the beholder's hair stiffened with agony, and his senses were strung to such a pitch of unearthly tension, that his ears, as he expressed it, seemed to open to his brain, and he heard the first footfall of his companion, who was then coming to relieve him, even as it touched the quay. He was found in a state of ineffable terror by his comrade, but the intruder upon his vigils had done its errand, and was gone.

These superstitions are rude, and coarse, and simple, but they illustrate the state of Scillonian life at the period when they occurred. It was an age of universal barbarism, when there was so little law, that the crew of a vessel, manned chiefly by Irish, landed, and having had a row with the islanders, swore to exterminate every soul in the place. The people fled in their boats, and the crew of a second vessel was brought on shore, and employed to reduce the Hibernians to submission. In those days, both here and in Cornwall, lanterns were fastened to the horns of cows, which were sent at night to the beach, as a beacon to mislead unwary pilots. Some of the tales, connected with these times, are terrible. In one case, a poor wretch, who had escaped from a wreck, and had clung fast to a rock, offered a large sum of gold to the crew of a boat from St. Agnes, as the price of his rescue. The children of St. Warna made him give his money up, and then left him to die. In another, a friend and associate, from the upsetting of his craft, had been flung into the sea, and had managed to swim to a point in the waves. His companions came near him, and threw out their grapnel, so as to swing round to the spot where he was. But the current ran strongly, the gale blew fiercely, and there seemed a good chance of losing their grapnel; so they hauled it up, and pulled away, and the poor fellow was, as they expected, drowned.   The men in the boat were of one family, and for this act, which was " un peu trop fort," even for St. Agnes, they got a surname, indicative of cruelty, which their descendants bear to this day.

There is in the South of France a place called Carpentras, the inhabitants of which are, what those of St. Agnes only were, barbarous and uncivilized.   I heard the other day a story of them, so very applicable to the Scilly of other and wilder days, as well as to its parsons, that I cannot help giving it here, premising that it loses half its force by not being told in a broad Languedocian dialect.

Le Curé de Carpentras, petit homme grêle et maigre, faisant un sermon à ses paroissiens, se plaignait de ce que, malgré ses instances reiterées, ils s'occupaient plus d'aller au cabaret, que d'apprendre leurs prières; et, dans son eloquence villageoise, et meridionale, il s'écria, " Savez vous ce qui arrivera de tout cela, mes frères ?   Le jour de jugement dernier, je serai dans un petit coin, et le bon Dieu me dira, ' Pist, pist, petit Curé de Carpentras, qu'avez vous fait de vos ouailles ?'   Savez vous ce que je lui repondrai ?   Non, vous ne le savez pas !   Eh bien, je lui dirai, ' Seigneur, bêtes vous me les avez donnés, bêtes je vous les rends.' "

I do not know whether Carpentras remains unchanged since the delivery of that sermon, but the difference wrought by the last few years in Scilly and the Scillonians is little less than miraculous.   I came hither, like every one else, full of prejudices, looking to find only a poor assemblage of fishermen, and prepared to pass a lenient judgment upon habits contrary to those of civilized life. I met with order, subordination, improvement, with progress unexpected as it was unexampled, and with a state of social and intellectual culture, strange indeed, and marvellous, in a place so lately abandoned to pauperism, and to crime. The shadow of Time has rested heavily upon these fair islands; the sea has conquered from them many a rood of smiling land; the dwellers on their shores waxed few and feeble; they became as it were the inheritance of the wild man, whose hand was against his fellow, and whose life was a life of violence and of blood. The dark and melancholy spirit of those days is fled, with the ignorance from which it sprung. All is now pleasantness and peace. In the midst of the comfort and prosperity so visible around, a Scillonian pastor might reverse the sarcasm of the Curé of Carpentras, and say truly of his flock, " Heureux vous me les avez donnés, heureux je vous les rends."

Appendix.

A SUPPLEMENTARY chapter is but a dull affair, after all. If anything good has gone before, this kind of parting word must always be full of melancholy. We are winding up a feast by languidly picking the bones. Yet a supplementary chapter must be written, were it only to rid the main narrative of those dry details and common-places, which, when gathered together and set apart from the rest, like an awkward squad, may be reviewed, and despatched at once.

In this case moreover I have an additional reason for dreading the ponderous dulness of an appendix. Almost every account of Scilly * has been written in a style so oracular and so heavy, with such a parade of learning, and such an apparent inquisition into antiquities, that as soon

---

* I may say here that Scilly is as much an unknown land as the Tierra del Fuego. In the city article of the Times of (I think) May 31st, it is contrasted with Lobos Afuero,—the guano rocks in the Pacific; and described as being inhabited by fishermen and pilots! I only wish the writer could see the Abbey gardens!

as one only touches on a point of classical or barbarian
information, the shadowy hand of some sage Theban seems
to start up and claim it for his own. Erudition* appears to
be the forte of the clerical historians of Scilly, their strongest
point, in fact, except smuggling. For my part, I suspect
the scholarship of these learned men, and grow tired of their
ancient Pegasus; even as the worthy Parisian, whose wife,
being in raptures with a statue in the Gardens of the
Tuilleries, exclaimed "Ah l'antique, comme c'est beau."
To which the spouse replied "Oui, ma femme, en marbre."

A friend of mine, who was Ambassador to the Sublime
Porte, was, once upon a time, sailing down the waters
of the Golden Horn in a cäique, having in his company
a French traveller, his temporary guest. My friend wrote
a very illegible hand. The conversation happening to turn
on the education of our diplomates, he observed, partly in
jest, partly also in reference to his own deficiencies as a
scribe, that England cared so little for the training of her
Ministers, as to employ—in his own case,—an Envoy who
could neither write nor spell. The Gaul bowed, shrugged
his shoulders, and made a note of the remark. And in

---

* If credit is sometimes taken where there is no learning, credit is
sometimes also denied where it exists. We know the old epigram,—

> "Ci gît Voltaire, que n'était rien,
> Pas même Acadamicien."

But I remember a case more in point. There is a college in Cambridge,
to which is accorded an easy and graceful præeminence in letters. Yet
a Cantab wrote this of one of its members,—

> "Here lies a Doctor of Divinity,
> And a senior Fellow of Trinity;
> And he knew as much, about Divinity,
> As any other Fellow of Trinity,"

his travels, produced with all that depth of observation and knowledge of other lands which is the characteristic of that thoughtful and sober nation, this little anecdote appeared, in so many words, as an instance of one among the many failings of England. Sometimes, when we are told that the Greeks must have colonized these islands, because Prigless is evidently a corruption of Pericles,* we are apt to feel such classical superiority rather overpowering, and to wish for an hour with an Ambassador not yet in his A B C.

> So brightly thy brain with its classics is burning,
> With Greek and with Latin, with verb and with tense,
> We whisper, oh give us a little less learning,
> And fill up the void with a little more sense.

But still, however I may linger on its confines, the supplementary chapter must be written, and, to use Falstaff's metaphor, this " borrowing only lengthens it out." So I may as well begin at once, as I have been writing a good deal about Scilly, by inquiring what the word Scilly means.

First.—Nearly all the varieties of the name have the same root. With the exception of " Æstrymnides,"† as they were called by Festus Avienus, a poet who wrote " De oris

---

* I suspect that the Scillonians, when at a loss for a local designation, sometimes coin one. A very old man told me that Troutbeck engaged a guide to the different places, and wrote down their names as they were reported to him by his cicerone. On one occasion they came to a tall rock, upon which the sun was shining. The man, not knowing what else to say, boldly affirmed that it was the " sun rock," and so it stands in Troutbeck:—à propos of him, I saw at a farm, called London, a set of antique tea-spoons and a sugar-spoon, that had belonged to the historian, marked with his initials J. T.

† Woodley.

maritimis " (and not one word of whose works have I ever read), their appellation has been always pretty much the same. They were described as " insulæ Sillinæ, as Sigdeles or Silures, as Sulleh by the Britons, as Sorlingæ insulæ in Facciolati, as Sulley or Silley in ancient grants. I agree therefore with Mr. Augustus Smith, who is most competent to form an opinion on the subject, and with Davies Gilbert, that the derivation of all these names is to be found in the ancient British word " lilli," " silli," Anglicé " Conger."

Secondly.—With regard to their physical changes, and their successive inhabitants, there is a field for conjecture much wider, and unfortunately, much more difficult to get over. That the Phœnicians came here, there is little doubt. That they traded here is not improbable. But I do not believe that these were the Cassiterides, or the Hesperides, unless as being taken for a part of that unknown Britain, from which the ancients drew such vast mineral wealth.* This is not unlikely to have been the case, for the great distance of these coasts naturally rendered all knowledge of them imperfect. The early merchants who came here were not colonists, and could know but little of the country beyond its shores, and the spots at which they touched to barter and to refit.

The people dwelling here were probably Britons, with a slight intermixture of strangers. There is not one relic,

---

* Discoverers of a country make, very naturally, mistakes of this nature. Columbus thought the island of Hispaniola part of the main land, and then afterwards believed the continent of America to be an island. This is exactly a case in point.

not one single trace, of any Greek or Phœnician custom, building, or name to be found.* Every vestige of religion that we see—circle, barrow, and cromlech—all are Druidical, and every burial-place is British or Danish. The aboriginal doubtless was harried by the Saxon, and the Saxon by the Dane, and the Dane gave place to the Norman ; but all these were kinsmen of the great Indo-Germanic race, passing over, and covering the land, like successive waves of the same sea.

Thirdly.—As respects the physical changes said to have taken place, there is a good deal of room for hesitation. The islands have certainly varied much, even within the memory of man. Two fields at St. Mary's, that are now submerged, are still remembered to have been cultivated. Between Bryher and Samson, and Bryher and Tresco, and around Tean and St. Helen's, are seen the remains of hedges and of buildings. Vestiges of the kind are to be found in many places, now covered by the sea. St. Helen's, which is uninhabited, had formerly a church. St. Lide's (supposed, I know not why, to be Rat Island), is spoken of by Leland as a place " whare was grate superstition." The same venerable authority calls Trescaw, or Iniscaw, the largest of the islands, mentions its circumference as being between nine and ten miles, and adds that wild boars

---

* I have, however, stumbled on a fragment of a Roman road or pavement, on the old track across the hill from Holy Vale to Hugh Town. It passes by one of the most charming places on the islands, now called " Rocky Hill," but formerly " Brimstone Hill." It is just the ivy-grown cottage in which to spend a honey-moon. A very pretty and intelligent damsel, seeing a stranger pausing before the house, asked me in, with the usual courtesy and good breeding of every rank in Scilly.

roamed over it. Its extent therefore must have been double
what it is now, in fact, exactly what it would be, including
Bryher and Samson, and it must have had coverts for the
wild animals that ranged through it, which it does not
possess now.

Fourthly.—Again, tradition says that Scilly was once
united to the Land's-end by a tract of country called the
Lionesse, or, in Cornish, Lethowsow, containing one hundred
and forty churches and a vast population, and that this wide
district was sunk beneath the sea, by some violent convulsion of nature. Whitaker supports this opinion, and says
that fishermen have brought up windows and fragments of
building from the buried houses,* which is simply absurd,
for windows were not used in the little cone-shaped,
hive-like cots of those days. But the family of Trevilian
have a very curious legend, bearing on this point. They
relate that one of their ancestors had great possessions on
the Lionesse, or Lethowsow, and that, at the time of the
inundation, he saved himself by swimming to shore on a
white horse, in memory whereof the family bear a white
horse as their crest to this hour. Some authors gravely fix
this deluge as anterior to the time of Trajan, from internal
evidence.

In the present day, we are too apt to disregard and to hold
cheap tradition. Yet tradition is often a sure guide, when
History is nearly mute, and particularly in the case of any
great calamity or shock, such, for example, as the deluge,
the memory of which is preserved where records are silent.

---

* Several persons tell me that, at the Seven Stones, small diamond-
shaped panes, set in lead, and forming rude casements, have been found.

This is found true, especially in districts solitary or remote, as at Scilly, or in the Highlands of Scotland. I remember an instance of its accuracy, which is to the point here. Some men were boring for water, in the North, but failed to find it. An old shepherd who observed them, told them to try a place which he pointed out, for there was a belief handed down from father to son, that a well had formerly existed there. The workmen tried the spot indicated, and, at some distance from the surface, broke into an ancient well. Now it is beyond doubt that local tradition asserts, positively, the partial or entire connexion of Scilly with the main land. The fact is beyond dispute. It may be without foundation, but, right or wrong, it is an article of faith, held most implicitly. A person with whom I was conversing one evening told me that people could once go from hence to Penzance, without finding on their way more water than a horse could drink up. There is likewise a popular legend, which relates that at the Seven Stones, where is now the light-ship, a city formerly stood.* It is a very curious circumstance that the part of the rock, which is pointed out by tradition as the site of this place, *is still called " the town."* In fact, I could fill a volume with the anecdotes relating to this subject, and to the subsidence of the land, followed by a proportionate advance of the waters. I heard from the grandson of a very aged man that his great grandfather remembered a causeway from the Abbey Church at Tresco across the downs, and along what is now sea, to the old Church at St. Helen's. There was a bridge

* It is always reported by the natives to have been called the " City of Lions."

across the Abbey pool, exactly on the same spot where the wooden one now stands.

Now that there have been great changes in the outward conformation of these lands is, I think, self-evident. People did not build under the sea. That portion, on which are seen works of man's raising, must, at the time of their erection, have been above the level of the ocean. Probably many of these changes have been wrought gradually and insensibly, as some of them must have taken place since the time of Leland, in the sixteenth century. A payment of seven quarters of wheat is mentioned, temp. Edward the Third, which proves that corn was then grown here, far more extensively than now. The sea is certainly encroaching slowly but steadily on all the western coasts, as well as here, for seventy years ago people played at cricket on green fields, between Marazion and Penzance, where there is now nothing but sand, under the level of the tides. But tradition, which often bears down in its current a sad memory of events that would otherwise have been forgotten, as History deems them beneath her notice, speaks so positively, and has always so spoken, of great and mysterious changes wrought hereabouts by some shock or convulsion, that I can hardly doubt that something of the kind must have occurred. In this case we can but guess at truth. Crests have not existed more than about six hundred years. Perhaps the white horse of the Trevilians may enable us to fix the date of these vast changes.

It is supposed that about the close of the eleventh century, there occurred, simultaneously, over all the coasts of England, a terrible invasion of the sea. It is known, at least, that, in many places, large tracts of land were entirely overflowed and lost. The great district, now called the Goodwin Sands, was certainly swallowed up at that period. Of this there can be no doubt, since it is an historical fact. It is equally capable of proof, I believe, that the whole of Mount's-bay was then submerged, the former line of coast having extended from Cudden point to Mousehole. The inundation in Kent and Sussex is known to have taken place in autumn. And in digging below the sands in Mount's-bay, leaves and hazel-nuts are constantly found, showing that the incursion of the sea must have been sudden, and at a season of the year when leaves and ripe fruits were plentiful. St. Michael's Mount was called "the hore rock in the wood," which it then was. The same deluge, that was so wide and so disastrous in its effects, may have proved equally fatal here. There might have been no Lionesse overwhelmed, and the tale may, as is said, be an invention of Florence of Worcester, but the deadly work of the waters not improbably left marks of its course on these islands. There was at that time a mighty flood. It submerged almost provinces. One portion of land, and no inconsiderable one, so destroyed, was in this very neighbourhood. Why may the effects of the deluge not have swept past this spot, and covered what evidently was once dry and cultivated land? Tradition is seldom wrong in outlines, though it is seldom right in details. The white horse of the Trevilians may not have been a mere myth, after all. When that flood took place along the coasts, their ancestor may have saved himself by swimming, and his son or grandson have assumed the present crest of the family,

in honour of an event which occurred within the memory
of living men.

"Gentlemen," said once a celebrated geologist, having
started some novel theory, before a crowded University
lecture room, and being afraid of his own boldness. "Gentlemen, I never theorise. Pray tell nobody what I have
now said."

In venturing on the above hypothesis, I do not lay down
a positive fact. Like the worthy lecturer, I state no theory.
I only throw out a suggestion, which, as I write entirely
from memory, and without any aid from books, may be
incorrect, both as to facts and dates. Perhaps, however,
the hint is worth giving, as it is the only practical way—at
least the only one that has occurred to me—of reconciling
mythology with what is authentic and true.

Fifthly.—The greater extent of these islands at some
former and uncertain time is, I think, proved, as well by
the scanty historical records, as by the Druidical remains,
and the sepulchral monuments, which are not only numerous,
but in many cases large and of some pretension. As I said
elsewhere, if there were temples, there must have been
priests, and worshippers. If there were so many chiefs
and men of rank (as we may suppose there were by the
large tombs so frequently discovered), there must also have
been common people in proportion. Now tombs of all
kinds are found everywhere. I saw by mere chance, at the
Abbey, two opened, evidently Danish, in one of which the
body had been doubled up, perhaps from being neglected
until cold, for the head was upon the chest. They both
pointed east and west. Several layers of bones were found

a day or two after, in one of which was a curious round stone, marked with a Greek cross, showing probably that the dead were Christians, and proving a successive population on this spot. They might have been a memento of the conquest of Scilly, in 927, by Athelstan, the eighth Saxon King, who, after offering up his orisons at the ancient Church of St. Buryan, near the Land's-end, came hither, and founded a priory on this sunny slope. On his return to Cornwall, he built also, in pursuance of his vow, a College at St. Buryan. There must have been some considerable number of inhabitants here, or a King would not have thought it worth his while to conduct the invasion in person. As regards the graves, Pliny certainly speaks of the fondness of our ancestors for insular interment, but the custom entailed an expense only to be incurred by the rich, and could not at all events be applicable to close and crowded burial places.

Another peculiarity in these islands, as I before said, is their want of all mediæval remains. There are literally no sepulchral relics. We find historical reminiscences of many families, some of considerable antiquity; but all are gone, and vanished utterly. The noble Norman house of de Barentin was seated here; and we read of Ranulph de Blankminster, and John de Allet, and William le Poer, and of others of no mean estate, yet there is no sign nor token of their existence to be discovered. I do not think that—except in the buried cities of America—there is on record an instance of such an utter blank, of such a complete loss of all human memories. The physical changes that have taken place, through the encroachments of the sea, do not account for this perfect void, nor for the fact that though this group has been peopled, and thickly peopled, even from times wholly mythical, we find nothing more recent than Druidical or Danish graves, until we come to those constructed for the fathers of living men. This gap in the ordinary course of time could not fail to strike so careful and acute an observer as Borlase, though he was utterly unable to account for the phœnomenon.

Sixthly.—The subsequent history of the islands may be comprised in a few words.

Of their ecclesiastical annals little is known. Their religious establishments were, it appears, many, but of small extent. There was a Priory at Tresco, dedicated to St. Nicholas, and communicating, by a road then over dry land, with a church at St. Helen's. We find records of cells or chapels, bearing the names of St. Theona, St. Kumon, or St. Rumon, St. Warna, and St. Mary.* There are likewise traces of similar institutions in other parts, as at Holy Vale, Church-ledge, Monk's Port, and Carn-Friars. On Sallakee down are two crosses, built into a hedge. But where, we may ask, are the relics of mediæval Catholicism? They are gone, even as it were a tale that is told. They exist only in a few grey stones at St. Helen's, in a solemn

---

* I discovered the site of one of these in Hugh Town, at the foot of the hill, leading to the Garrison. Within the memory of man there was standing a doorway, with a fine pointed arch, and some windows, whose copings and mullions were of carved stone. My informant told me that she lived in it, and that her father remembered it as an "old Roman Church." Its remains were only pulled down twenty years ago, for I spoke with the mason who did it. Some of the sculptured stones may still be seen on the spot. The burial-ground was above it, on the rising ground. Lying against the wall, at the old Pier, may be seen the ancient money-box of the Church. It is identified by several persons, and is still entire.

arch at Tresco, in the spirit that broods over the heath at Sallakee, and clings around the neglected crosses that are mouldering there. All that we see is no more than this. All that we know is that Scilly was granted, according to one account, by Athelstan the Saxon, to the Abbey of Tavistock; and, according to another, to the same Abbey, by Henry the First. The principal seat of spiritual government was at Tresco, and the head of it was called the Prior of Scilly. At the Reformation it lapsed to the Crown.

As to its civil state, Sulley, or Silley, was granted by Henry the First, to Reginald de Dunstanville, Earl of Cornwall, his illegitimate son, and was governed, in general, by the Coroner, as his deputy. It seems to have been always attached to the Earldom of Cornwall, as, for its sins, it now is to the Duchy. Law, however, appears to have partaken of the character of those good old times.

For example, by the Rolls " Placita de juratis et assisis," 12th of Edward the First,—

" John de Allet, and Isabella his wife, hold the Isle of Scilly, and hold there all kind of pleas of the Crown, throughout their jurisdiction, and make indictments of felonies. When any one is attainted of any felony, he ought to be taken to a certain rock in the sea, and with two barley loaves, and one pitcher of water upon the same rock, they leave the same felon, until, by the flowing of the sea, he is swallowed up ! "

This John de Allet held lands of Ranulph de Blankminster,* Constable of the Castle of Ennour,† by Knight's

---

* Called in the old rolls, de Blanco ministerio, Blankminster, or Whitchurch.

† Ut ante, En-mour, Inys-more, *i. e.* Great island, St. Mary's.

service. In the time of Henry the Third, Dreux de Barentin was the great man here. They were true sea kings, those old Barentins, keeping to the tastes of the Northmen. They held the Channel Islands, under the Crown, and were known to have stuck, as long as they could, to the sea-shore.

After this time, the Isles of Scilly were " minished and brought very low, by persecution, and plague, and trouble." In the time of Henry the Sixth, they were valued only at a rent of fifty puffins, or 6s. 8d. In 1484, temp. Richard the Third, they were estimated, " in time of peace, at 40s., in time of war, nothing." At the Reformation, they are said to have been forgotten! They did not go with the Abbey of Tavistock, to which they pertained ecclesiastically, nor were they placed under the jurisdiction of the Bishop of Exeter till 1837.* In fact, it is a mystery how or when the Civil and Ecclesiastical power lapsed to the Duchy of Cornwall. In the grant of it to the King's eldest son, there is no mention whatever made of the Isles of Scilly.†

On the twentieth of June, 6th year of Edward the Sixth, in a deed of releasing an annuity,‡ granted by Beauchamp, out of lands in Trevenethick, in Saint Agnes parish, in Cornwall, the party releasing describes himself as " Thomas Godolghan, Esq., Captyn of the Iles of Scilley."

Queen Elizabeth granted these islands to Sir Francis Godolphin, on military tenure, at a yearly rent of £10, and they remained in his family till about seventeen years ago, when, the Duke of Leeds refusing to renew, William

---

* London Gazette, Aug. 24, 1838.   † Heath.   ‡ Sic.

the Fourth, as Duke of Cornwall, gave a lease for ninety-nine years, on three lives, to the present Proprietor, Mr. Augustus Smith.

Seventhly.—In my motto, prefixed to this work, I have altered the Gyara and Seripho of Juvenal into names derived from this group, and there is a propriety in doing so, for these islands, like those of Greece, were used as places of confinement, and of banishment.* Instantius, a heterodox Bishop from Spain, was exiled hither by the Emperor Maximus, and so were many Churchmen, and many lay Romans of rank. Dr. Bastwick, after his cruel treatment by the Star Chamber, was detained here as a prisoner till 1640. He was kept in Star Castle.

The next person immured was a curiosity.

Fifth Report of the Keeper of Public Records, 1655, 1656, p. 257 :—

"John Biddle, the celebrated Unitarian, a prisoner at Scilly, allowed a pension of 10s. per week, and imprisoned there by Oliver Cromwell, *to keep him out of the way of his persecutors.*" †

What a commentary on the success of the struggle for religious liberty !

---

* Woodley.

† We know well the violence of polemical hate. Only fancy an assembly of the representatives of the different sects, who have found here a prison or a home. Only picture the Arian and Eutychian heresiarch matched with the Unitarian ; and the Independent, and the Fifth monarchy man, and John Wesley, as tough as any of them, in spite of his long white hair. I could find but one simile to express their meeting, and that is in a sermon I once heard by a worthy and learned Canon. He was describing the Resurrection. "My brethren," said the Reverend Demosthenes, "imagine a pile of bones, past all imagination ! "

In 1645 Prince Charles came here for six weeks. Lady Fanshawe, in her Memoirs, gives a delightful picture of the discomforts of an abode among the wreckers and smugglers of that day. Let it be remembered that the high-born Cavaliers and Ladies, then adhering to the royal cause, did so voluntarily. They might have submitted, and enjoyed their own in peace, but they preferred exile with honour. And when Sir John Grenville might have surrendered these islands to Van Tromp, who came with a mighty armament, and offered in exchange for them most advantageous terms, he utterly refused to treat with a stranger, or to yield up any part of the soil of England to foreign rule. After a gallant struggle, he gave up the place into the hands of Blake and Ayscough, the rebel leaders, in May, 1651.

Scilly was the resort of many of the distressed Cavaliers, who found here a temporary asylum. Among them was a gentleman of the family of the Lord Proprietor, Francis Godolphin, "father probably of the famous Sydney Godolphin." There are, at Tresco Abbey, some very interesting fragments of letters, written by him during his residence. They give such a faithful picture of the state of affairs then existing in the islands, that I cannot refrain from transcribing portions of them, which I am permitted to do, by the kindness of their owner. They all bear the date of 1643.

" *From Francis Godolphin to John Rogers.*

" For your coming over and making up your books, if it were not for displeasing somebody that I never will if I can helpe it, I should be very glad of seeing you, and the place

is worth your seeing too ; indeed I like it, much better than
I did expect, though I must confess I came much the more
willingly hither, because I was not well at ease where I was."

* * * * *

" There has noe ship come in hither since Jack went, but a
Falmouth warrier,* which received a broadside from one of
the Parl. ships the day before.

" I conceive there can be no possibility of peace. Our
God be merciful to us.

" Your friend,

" FRA. GODOLPHIN.

" I pray you lett there be one line in your next in another
hand."

No. 2.   *From Scilly*

* * * " to come hither, considering how glad I am
at all hours to have you by me, and the novelty of the place
for a few days would entertain you contentedly enough,
and more than a few would tire you ten times more than
Compton did. There are also some things about this place,
I doe not mean the fortifications, but the grounds, wherein
your judgment, having viewed it, would be of use to me.
I would also that you should see my patience, for this place,
in respect of an absolute want of all welcome company, is
a strange change to me.

" Yet a very honest man, born here, may live very
happily, as many doe, that would not change for twice soe
much a year in Cornwall.

---

* Sic.

" For all this, I would by noe means be guilty of drawing you hither, if it any way dislike your best friend. We have seen noe doubtful ship upon the coast a great while.

*   *   *   *   *

                              " Yours,

" 13th June, 1643."   " F. G.

No. 3.

" I have received a warrant from the King to carry over two hundred men, more, for the safeguard of the fort at Silly; for the Summer, the estates of divers delinquents, and the tithes of divers parishes, are directed towards the maintenance of the place.

" There are also the woods of some delinquents, as the Lord Robartes, both Trevills, Boscawen, Seynt Aubin, and Erisey(?), appointed to be sold, by Mr. Jane, Mr. Dryden, Mr. Spemon, out of which £600 is, in the first place, to be paid to me, for provision of a magasin of victualls at Silly."

In the margin is added,—

" All the news at Oxford is, of the great blow the Scotts have had from my Ld. of Newcastle, six thousand said to be slain, and taken, with all their ordinance and ammunition; this came to the King by many several wayes, and I am confident is true in a great measure, which God grant, to His glory, and our comfort, but there is noe express come yet from the army."

No. 4. Fragment.

"The army goes on; the men from Cornwall are putt
over for one month more, I must be heer at midsomer, being
then promised fairly money for Silly, without which I dare
not goe amongst them. If I speed well, I shall, God
willing, be with you, soe as that I may be returned from
Silly by Michaelmas.

"Your friend,

"June 20th." "Fra. Godolphin.

In Lady Fanshawe's Memoirs (London, 1831, pp. 74, 75),
March 1645, after giving an account of her misfortunes
during the passage with Sir Nicholas Crispe,* she says,—

"Next day, after having been pillaged, and extremely
sick, and big with child, I was set on shore almost dead in
the Island of Scilly. When we had got to our quarters
near the Castle, where the Prince lay, I went to bed, which
was so vile, that my footman ever lay in a better, and we
had but three in the whole house, which consisted of four
rooms, or rather partitions, two low rooms, and two little
lofts, with a ladder to go up; in one of these they kept
·dried fish, which was his trade, and in this my husband's
two clerks lay, one there was for my sister, and one for
myself, and one among the rest of the servants. But when
I waked in the morning, I was so cold I knew not what to
do; but the daylight discovered that the bed was near
swimming with the sea, which the owner told us afterwards

---

* Is this the good and loyal merchant, so celebrated in the civil wars?

it never did so but at spring-tide. With this we were destitute of clothes, and meat, and fuel, and truly we begged our daily bread, for we thought every meal our last."

In 1669 the Grand Duke Cosmo, who was making a tour of Great Britain, came to Scilly. He gives, in his diary, a view of Star Castle, as it then existed, which corresponds pretty closely with its appearance at the present day. The Grand Duke speaks in terms of praise of the islands, and of the reception he met with from the Governor.

After the Great Rebellion we find the islands declining gradually. The steward of the Godolphin family* was the virtual master, and, like all stewards, fattened on the spoils of his lord. Old Troutbeck gives a lamentable picture of the treatment of all who differed from this functionary, and of the neglect of the Leeds family. A petition sent up by him as Chaplain, to the Duchess of Leeds, was returned by her, and an answer read in Church, *by the clerk*, to the intent, " that the Duchess supposed the signatures to the paper she had received forgeries, and that she never inter-

---

* I insert here an anecdote, very honourable to the nobleman, then Proprietor.   The common ancestor of the present families of the name of Sherris was drowned, and his vessel lost. He left a widow, a son who was quite a youth, and six daughters. The boy, feeling his mother and sisters dependent on him, and unable to pay his rent, boldly went to England, and saw Lord Godolphin. He was " fair and of a ruddy countenance." When he had told his sad tale, he was dismissed with the simple words, " Well, my flaxen-haired boy, go back as fast as you can to Scilly." There was, however, a generous eloquence in his Lord's brevity.   He received his house and land, rent free, for his life, and was also appointed to a place in the Customs. The five girls, who survived, were insular heiresses, for it is related that they had fortunes of " six score guineas " each. They, too, behaved very well. The uncle's will, under which they inherited this wealth, left it only to four, by name. Those four, nevertheless, refused to profit by what they said must have been a mistake. They made their sister's share equal to their own.

fered in the Duke's business." Poor old Troutbeck, though he did run away to escape the consequences of a little smuggling, wrote a very amusing book, which is well worth the trouble of reading by any one, who wishes to compare the state of Scilly in his time with its position now.

The next visitor to St. Mary's was no Cavalier. In 1743, in Wesley's Journal, I find that he started from St. Ives, with three companions, in a boat borrowed from the Mayor. They diverted their attention from the dangers of the sea by singing an appropriate psalm. On landing at St. Mary's, he called on the Governor, and presented him with a newspaper (just as one does at the Cape, or at Calcutta, now). Not being allowed to preach in the Church, he held forth twice, in the street, to a great crowd, among whom he distributed tracts and hymn-books. He then returned, and was in some peril, but reached St. Ives safely.

Two rather naive and characteristic remarks are added by the excellent Missionary.

First.—When the pilot, from the heavy swell, said that they should be lucky if they reached land, Mr. Wesley remarked " that he knew not Him whom the wind and seas obey."

Secondly.—When he saw the numbers of workmen and people employed by Government, he marvelled " at their being collected on such a barren rock, which whosoever would take might have for his pains," but he discovered, as a reason, *the opportunity of hearing the Gospel from him.*

I learn, however,—though the fact is suppressed by the worthy man,—that he was pelted out of Hugh Town, and that this was the reason of his short stay.

There now remains little to add. The state of Scilly began at this time to reach its lowest point of depression. St. Agnes was at one period entirely uninhabited. The wretched dwellers on the other islands used to come to St. Mary's, every Saturday, for the purpose of systematic beggary; and the pittance thus gained, with a trifle earned by burning kelp, and by fishing, formed their sole resource. Their condition * may be supposed from this fact. So it is no wonder that in 1774 the court rolls show the existence of great misery, which continued, for many years, to grow worse and worse, until, in 1818, a deputation from the magistrates at Penzance came over to investigate it. They did so, to the best of their ability. On the publication of their report, which excited a painful feeling, very similar to that now awakened for the suffering and starving people of Skye, a subscription was begun throughout England on their behalf, and nearly ten thousand pounds were raised for their relief. A collection of this kind generally starts with enthusiasm, and ends in a job. It was so in this instance. The money found its way into the wrong pockets. " Corporations," said Lord Thurlow, " are things that have neither noses to pull, nor bodies to kick;" and the same may be said of committees. The amount, thus liberally given, disappeared in the apparent

---

* It is much to the credit of the Scillonians that, in one respect, their standard of morality is very high. They are extremely honest. In all my dealings with them, I have never met with one attempt at fraud. A person who has the reputation of being at all lax, in this respect, is looked down upon, and shunned, and is made a sort of Pariah among his neighbours. The same feeling that leaves doors unbarred, and linen exposed on the hills to bleach, at night, is extended to personal immunity from danger. Not only a man, but a girl, may walk about in safety, at any hour, without the slightest fear of insult, or of wrong.

attempt to establish a pilchard fishery; and the distress remained, as deeply rooted and as hopeless, as before.

In 1810, Mr. Tucker, Surveyor General of the Duchy of Cornwall, came to Scilly, to consider, and report on, the practicability of making a roadstead and harbour. His pamphlet shows much ability, and contains many valuable suggestions; but though he warmly advocated the construction of extensive works, as a place of refuge for the shipping, his advice met with no attention from the government.

The population, in 1801, was 1,813; in 1838,—2,618.

In the census of 1851, the numbers were,—

St. Mary's
Males 737   Houses.
Females 905   285
                 —1642

Tresco
Males 177
Females 239   96
                  — 416

St. Martin's
Males 97
Females 114   46
                  — 211

Bryher and Samson
Males 68
Females 60   33
                  — 128

St. Agnes
Males 83
Females 121   51
                  — 204

Total Souls.... 2,601 .. Houses 511

The females appear more numerous than the males, but this is merely owing to the absence of the latter with their ships, both as pilots, and as being engaged in the foreign trade. And the seeming diminution of the population is caused by a stop having been put to the ruinous and demoralising subdivision of land,* which was carried to such a frightful extent, that sons and daughters were portioned off with a few square yards of ground.

The whole group of Scilly consists of one hundred and forty-five rocks, but the inhabited portions at present are but six in number, as will be seen by the statement above.   Many islands, formerly cultivated and peopled, are now deserted.

By the kindness of Mr. John Banfield, I have obtained correct returns of the shipping, at three periods, equidistant from each other, and sufficiently remote to give a good idea of the steady and increasing prosperity of the port.

---

* My long residence in France enables me to speak on this point sadly and decidedly.   The law of majorats, or of primogeniture, has been repealed in that country about sixty years.   The effect anticipated from its abolition was the creation of an independent class of small proprietors, such as now exists in Italy, where the Code civile has been a less time in operation.   But France has *passed through that stage*, and has gone a step lower in the scale.   Land is there parcelled out into portions so minute, and so numerous, as hardly to be imagined by us ; but it is done to such an extent that even the roads and paths form a subject of enormous litigation, and of vast importance.   And as every Frenchman wishes to be a proprietor, the first thing done by a peasant, when he gets a little money, is to buy a patch of land, paying part of the purchase-money, and borrowing the remainder on mortgage,   An idea of the growing ruin of this great class may be formed from the fact that the lowest average rate of interest, for capital raised on this species of security, is nine per cent ; while the whole debt, on the landed property of France, is not less than four hundred and fifty millions sterling, and I have heard it, on good authority, computed at five hundred millions !

On the 31st of December, 1825, there belonged to Scilly, eleven vessels under 50 tons, four vessels above 50 tons;—total, fifteen vessels, of the burthen of 574 tons.

On the 31st of December, 1838,—twenty vessels under fifty tons, thirty vessels above fifty tons;—total, fifty vessels, of the burthen of 3,062 tons.

On the 31st of December, 1851,—thirteen vessels under fifty tons, forty-six vessels above fifty tons; — total, fifty-nine vessels, of the burthen of 6,843 tons.

The largest vessel built at, and belonging to, the port, is the " Cassiterides," of 414 tons register, belonging to the Messrs. Banfield. A great proportion of the Scillonian merchantmen is A. 1. for twelve years, at Lloyd's. In a dozen years the average measurement increased from sixty-one, to one hundred and sixteen tons; a progress, probably, unparalleled in the annals of maritime enterprise.

If Scilly owed to the present Proprietor no more than the abolition of this system, she would have entailed upon her a deep debt of gratitude. But her obligations are far more extensive and important, and she has forgotten the sufferings caused by her ancient misrule, and has thriven under a hand dispensing far more liberally than it receives.

If the scene of more than Celtic misery which, seventeen years ago, characterized these islands, has, like the magic of a dissolving view, passed into a state of prosperity without a parallel; if there be no mendicancy, no Unions, and no paupers; if the land be cultivated like a garden, and the port full of ships; if the churches be crowded with well dressed, and devout, congregations ; if smuggling and wrecking be unknown; if all these things be true, and, that they are so, every resident can testify, it is wholly the work of one man, in spite of every obstacle, and discouragement, and long standing abuse !

He may, indeed, well say, as did his namesake of Rome,—

"LATERITIAM · INVENI · MARMOREAM · RELINQUO." *

---

* I found it of brick, I leave it of marble.

PRINTED BY F. T. VIBERT. MARKET PLACE, PENZANCE.

ERRATA.

Page 5, line 6, *for* voilá, *read* voilà.

  „ 48, Note, *for* byzigean, *read* byrigean.

  „ 72, line 23, after " Marie " insert a comma.

  „ 143, line 13, after " Edwin " insert a comma.

  „ 158, 4th line from bottom, *for* siezing, *read* seizing.

  „ 172, line 14, *for* Sant-aspery-neck, *read* Sant-aspery neck.

  „ 199. Note, *for* Afuero, *read* Afuera.

  „ 223, line 18, *for* this system. *read* the old system.

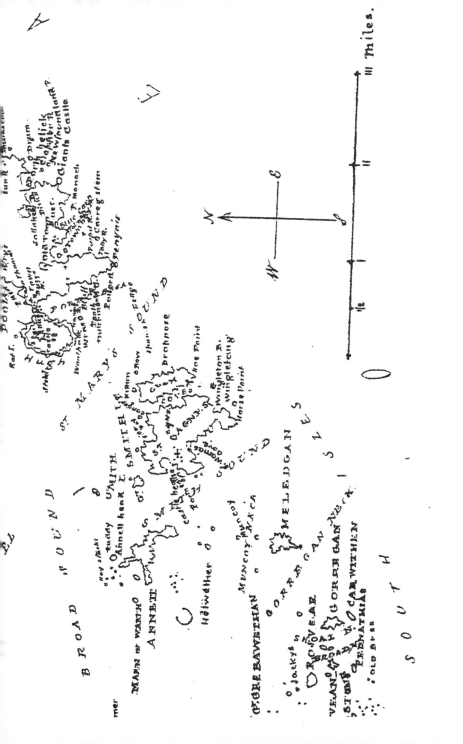

Also published by Llanerch:

POPULAR ROMANCES
OF THE WEST COUNTRY:
THE TRADITIONS &c
OF OLD CORNWALL
by Robert Hunt.

TRADITIONS AND HEARTHSIDE
TALES OF WEST CORNWALL .
by W. Bottrell.

BRITISH GOBLINS:
THE REALM OF FAERIE
by Wirt Sikes.

SYMBOLISM OF THE
CELTIC CROSS
by Derek Bryce.

A HISTORY OF THE
KINGS OF ENGLAND
by Simeon of Durham.

For a complete list, write to Llanerch Publishers, Felinfach, Lampeter, Dyfed, SA48 8PJ.